THOMIST REALISM
AND THE
CRITIQUE OF KNOWLEDGE

ETIENNE GILSON

THOMIST REALISM
AND THE
CRITIQUE OF KNOWLEDGE

TRANSLATED BY MARK A. WAUCK

IGNATIUS PRESS   SAN FRANCISCO

Title of the French original:
*Réalisme thomiste et critique
de la connaissance*
© 1939, 1983 Librairie Philosophique J. Vrin
Paris, France
http://www.vrin.fr

Cover image:
Saint Thomas Aquinas
Fra Angelico (1387–1455)
1440–1442. Mural, 108 × 145 cm.
Museo di S. Marco, Florence, Italy
© Erich Lessing / Art Resource, New York

Cover design by Roxanne Mei Lum

Republished in 2012 by Ignatius Press
© 1986 by Ignatius Press, San Francisco
All rights reserved
ISBN 978-1-58617-685-3
Library of Congress Control Number
Printed in the United States of America ∞

CONTENTS

FOREWORD

"When two or more independent insights cross a new philosophy is born." Etienne Gilson would probably have approved of this sage observation of his teacher, Henri Bergson, but he might have denied that the dictum applied to his own life. Insistent throughout his career that he was first and foremost an historian of philosophy, Gilson understood his task to be one of restoration, restoration of an imperfectly understood medieval tradition of Christian thought, but principally the restoration of the wisdom of the Common Doctor of the Church, St. Thomas Aquinas. Nonetheless, this lifelong task involved Gilson in forging a strikingly original synthesis, one crafted in the catalyst of that history of philosophy to which he gave so lovingly his genius and his amazing erudition.

If existence is the unity in which all essences are annealed in being, as Gilson's master, Aquinas, taught, then the very existence of Gilson's personal philosophical synthesis was fashioned principally by three distinct convictions. Any one of them would have made Gilson a formidable figure in twentieth-century thought, but the unity of the three made Gilson, in my judgment, the most striking single figure in Catholic thought in this century. Gilson's first conviction was his insistence that there exists in fact a philosophical tradition that must be denominated Christian because it

7

grew within and was nourished by the Catholic faith. From being to possibility is a valid inference, and hence any abstract isolation of philosophy from Christianity is a futile exercise in misplaced logic. Christian philosophy exists, and when we study it historically we discover a body of teaching vastly superior to its classical antecedents and to its modern successors.

The test, Gilson insisted, was the reality of history itself. That "Christian philosophy" is a dubious concept, as Gilson's adversaries have argued, is a pretension easily countered by his own insistence that concepts must be measured by reality and not the other way around. Gilson's profound Aristotelian realism exercised in his long critique against Cartesian rationalism found here a striking illustration of its epistemological power. By their fruits ye shall know them! Let those who deny that philosophy can be Christian explain away a millenium of speculation which simply would never have been had Christendom not existed.

To the reality of the history of Christian philosophy can be added Gilson's second affirmation: that the critical problem from which rationalism and idealism emerged was never posed by St. Thomas Aquinas because his realism rendered the so-called "problem of knowledge" at best superfluous and at worst a betrayal of the first principles of Thomistic realism. Whether philosophy, especially first philosophy or metaphysics, ought to begin with a critique of knowledge or not is a logically coherent question, but it cannot be answered in the affirmative by men claiming to speak in the name of St. Thomas Aquinas. History, once again history, instructs us that the same Aquinas did not begin to philosophize as though he were a post-Cartesian. Aquinas did not commence with a universal doubt concerning the capacity of human intelligence to know the real not because St. Thomas did not know Descartes but because any variant on the universal doubt as well as the doubt itself cancels the first principles of metaphysical or Thomistic realism.

If the immediate evidence of sensation, penetrated by the intellect, yields a universe of things existing in independence of our knowing them, then the Thomistic realism of the fact of existence opens the gate to the Thomistic metaphysics of the primacy of the act of existing in being. Delineated somewhat hesitantly in *God and Philosophy*, Gilson's rediscovery of the central role of existence in St. Thomas was first hammered home in the chapter "Existence and Reality" added to the fifth edition of his *Le Thomisme*. These insights were expanded brilliantly in his monumental *Being and Some Philosophers* and later were recapitulated in his shorter *The Spirit of Thomism*. It should come as no surprise that history orchestrated this finale to Etienne Gilson's metaphysical synthesis. The book of Exodus is not a metaphysics: it is the revealed Word of God. But although not a metaphysics, Exodus is an invitation to reasonable men to fashion a metaphysics of the Name of God. If the Name of God is Being, "I Am Who Am", then to create means to make things be. Their very existence is the core of their being, that without which they would be nothing. The central importance of *esse* in the full sweep of St. Thomas' thought seemed to have been missed, although never quite denied, by the majority of Aquinas' most illustrious commentators. Gilson often puzzled over this curious anomaly and Gilson's discovery reminds me of Chesterton's definition of paradox: you must suddenly begin to see white on black for the first time after having seen black on white all your life.

The metaphysics of being as existence crowned Gilson's

earlier insistence on the reality of Christian philosophy. Here we find a perfectly rational doctrine, indeed — insist its supporters — the only fully rational doctrine about being, which was primed by the historical revelation of God to Moses. Both the Christian origin of the teaching and the preeminent role granted existence in turn bend back and support the immediate realism of Aquinas, a realism beginning with the truth that things are and that I know them to be because I sense and perceive them. The touchstone of existence is, as the innocent pun suggests, sensation. In knowing immediately that which is, man knows the effect of him who simply Is. *This* truth man does *not* know immediately: he must prove it by process of subsequent reasoning, but a reasoning that takes its point of departure from a world of material things that is later known to be God's creation. Whether we *could* have known all this outside the context of Christian history is an unreal question because in fact we have known this wisdom only within that history. Nobody outside Christianity has known it at all. Gilson often seemed slightly impatient with adversaries who could not see what appeared to him to be clairvoyantly evident. In their defense we should point out that Gilson spent many years in careful research and original speculation before discovering what, once discovered, then seemed to him to be obvious. He ended where he began: with what the catechism taught him as a child.[1]

The appearance of this English translation of Etienne Gilson's *Réalisme thomiste et critique de la connaissance* by Mr. Mark Wauck closes what has certainly been the most significant gap in the corpus of Gilson's writings published in English. At the risk of offending enthusiasts of Gilson who

[1] See E. Gilson, *The Philosopher and Theology,* for an extended development of this theme.

might be fond of this or that book in French which has not
found its way into English, I suggest—along with Mr.
Wauck—that *Thomist Realism and the Critique of Knowledge*
has been *the* Gilson work whose availability in English has
been most sorely missed. Written as a definitive answer
to those philosophers who sought to reconcile critical philosophy with scholastic realism, it is the groundwork for
the later works in which Gilson plumbed the depths of St.
Thomas' teaching on existence and judgment. Having firmly
established a "realism of knowledge", thus freeing realism
from the excess critical baggage with which it had been
burdened, in the final chapter he began his metaphysical
journey to the heart of reality, the act of existence. It is no
coincidence that *Réalisme thomiste* preceded *Being and Some
Philosophers*, for it was during his historical study of the
various critical realisms then current that Gilson became increasingly aware that a faulty understanding of the word
"existence" was the cause for so much of the philosophical
wreckage on the stage of history. Time and again Gilson
had turned to history to deepen his understanding of existence, and in *Réalisme thomiste* history became the crucible
in which his timeless insights into Thomist metaphysics
were tempered. In *Being and Some Philosophers* those insights
received their mature expression. No serious student of
either St. Thomas or Etienne Gilson can afford to impoverish himself by not mastering the book here being
introduced.

I use the word "impoverish" advisedly. Gilson's overarch-
ing intention was to return his own readers to the text of St.
Thomas in order that they might ponder that text in independence of subsequent commentary and interpretation.
Yet in this very endeavor Gilson himself necessarily became
a latter-day commentator: necessarily, because the modern

student of philosophy is separated from St. Thomas not only by time-conditioned modes of expression but more importantly by frequently unconscious presuppositions concerning the very nature of philosophy which are deterrents to a full and correct appreciation of St. Thomas' doctrine. Being faithful, I trust, to Gilson's insistence that there is a unity of philosophical experience and that philosophers cannot be understood as philosophers unless understood in the context of their own historical moment and in relationship to their influences, I submit that Gilson's own road to the wisdom of St. Thomas is of compelling importance to the history of philosophy and hence to philosophical progress, including, of course, the progress of Thomism as a living doctrine. Anything less than this attitude would be pure philosophical archaism, the illusion of late twentieth-century men who pick up books written hundreds and possibly even a pair of millenia earlier and who think they can understand them the better the more they ignore everything else written about them. The arrogance is too obvious for commentary, but the arrogance in question is one that Gilson opposed all his life, beginning with his insistence that Descartes must be read in the context of the scholastic and medieval vocabulary he pressed into the service of his philosophical revolution.

Réalisme thomiste was published in 1939 by a man who had not come out of the traditional mold of Catholic philosophical scholarship which dominated the Europe of his time. Etienne Gilson had neither the benefits nor the defects of a "Catholic education". All of his teachers and his entire university education were secular. Gilson backed into the medieval tradition due to his early interest in Descartes. In fact it was at the behest of Lucien Lévy-Bruhl, no uncritical admirer of St. Thomas, that Gilson selected as the subject of his thesis the influence of medieval philosophy on Descartes, a project which led to the classic study *Etudes sur le rôle de la pensée médiévale dans la formation du système cartésien.* From these unpromising beginnings grew his lifelong commitment to medieval studies. Gilson's approach to St. Thomas was therefore uniquely personal and untraditional. He inherited none of the prejudices nor even the virtues of scholars and teachers, most of them clerics, who had been educated in scholasticism and whose lives had largely been spent in Catholic institutions. Gilson once confessed that he had not even heard of the encyclical *Aeterni patris* until long after he had taken up the banner of a specifically Christian philosophy and after he had spent years in working toward his own personal solution to the issues in question. Typical of Gilson's *anima naturaliter christiana* was his pleasant discovery that Leo XIII had much earlier said the same thing that Gilson had been saying, in an often bitter debate, to his fellow Catholic philosophers in France.

Ever since the Revolution of 1789, the Catholic sensibility had been dominated by a siege mentality. Gilson correctly saw that the revival of scholastic philosophy partook in great measure of this siege mentality and that this defensive attitude toward modern philosophy had led to a tendency to perceive philosophical issues as they had been framed by its adversaries rather than in the independent light of the scholastic tradition. As so often happens this siege mentality produced its own ape: a desperate desire to be philosophically respectable in a basically hostile and secularist world. At the time *Réalisme thomiste* was published, rationalism and idealism in a dozen forms had settled upon the mind of the academy. Perhaps Léon Brunschvicg best summed up the philosophical zeitgeist in a lapidary slogan: "Whatever cannot be reduced to reason is either nonexistent or unimportant." The school of Louvain, following the path opened by Cardinal Mercier,[2] was in the vanguard of the attempt to engage scholastic philosophy in a dialogue with the then contemporary rationalism. Scholasticism would sally forth to a field of its enemy's own choosing, accepting the challenge of the Cartesian doubt by subjecting knowledge to a critique which suspended, if only critically, man's spontaneous convictions about knowing a real world of existing things immediately present to experience. Critical realism still wanted Thomistic conclusions, but it wanted them to issue from a Cartesian or Kantian point of departure.

In *Le Réalisme méthodique,* a collection of articles which appeared between 1930 and 1935, published in book form in 1936, Gilson had attacked the critical realisms of Cardinal Mercier, late founder of the Institut Supérieur de Philosophie of Louvain, and Monsignor Léon Noël, student of and successor to Cardinal Mercier at the Institut Supérieur. Gilson's thesis was that realism was incompatible with the critical method and that realism, to the extent that it was reflective and aware of its guiding principles, was its own proper method. To the extent that Cardinal Mercier and Monsignor Noël submitted realism to the strictures of the critical method, their doctrine could not be considered realist.

Written in a lively, controversial style, *Le Réalisme méthodique* caused a very considerable stir among scholastic

[2] In 1882, in the wake of the encyclical *Aeterni patris* and as a result of a certain amount of pressure from Leo XIII himself, a chair of Thomistic philosophy was established at the Catholic University of Louvain, and the then Abbé Mercier was selected for the position. In 1889 the Institut Supérieur de Philosophie was established by a papal brief with Mercier as the first director. Over the years the Institut Supérieur and its "house organ", the *Revue néoscolastique de philosophie*, attained enormous prestige and exercised a profound influence as a leader in the revival of medieval philosophy.

philosophers, for Cardinal Mercier and Monsignor Noël were widely regarded as two of the foremost scholastic philosophers of the day and had contributed mightily to the resurgence of interest in scholastic philosophy. Gilson was attacked for everything from obscurantism to pragmatism, and Monsignor Noël himself wrote in defense of his own doctrine and that of Cardinal Mercier, maintaining that, to be properly philosophical, realism must be critical. The storm of criticism was so intense and the principles involved so important that Gilson felt constrained to respond.

Réalisme thomiste was his response, the response of a man who seemed genuinely surprised that putative Thomists found themselves constrained to answer the critical question. Some critical realists merely went through the motions of asking the critical question or did so without foreseeing the consequences; others embraced it with open eyes, well aware of the dangers involved. All such efforts indicated "a radical misconception of the uniqueness of pure philosophical principles and of the internal necessity linking principles and conclusions". This question, insisted Gilson, ought never to have been asked in the first place, at least not by men who claimed to be realists in the tradition of Thomas Aquinas. Gilson never attacked critical philosophy on any supposed internal contradiction. The critical method is a contradiction only within realism, because if we do not begin with things, if we begin with thought, then realism is not realism but something else. The realist is a philosopher who does not forget that he is a man when he begins to philosophize. As a man, if he be sane, a philosopher has not the faintest shade of a doubt that he exists in a world of things existing in independence of his cognition; even more, the very data of that knowing tell him that knowing is of being and not of knowing; in turn, he knows all this, not because of some privileged intuition into a supposedly substantive *cogito,* but because he, as a flesh and blood human being, could not judge otherwise if he tried, unless —and only unless, Gilson insisted—he deliberately isolated his mind from his body. Gilson, with his characteristic French irony, granted any philosopher the right to undertake this unnatural surgery should he so desire. But when such a philosopher has made it, he has ceased philosophizing as the man he was before he began to philosophize, and he has lost the right, by an imperative of logic itself, to call himself a realist.

As always, Gilson adopts an historical approach. With a firm hand he paints the eighteenth- and nineteenth-century background, the first attempts of non-scholastic philosophers to come to grips with the critical problem, and the influence men like Thomas Reid had on neo-scholastic epistemology in the nineteenth and early twentieth centuries. The result is a masterful account of the various forces that shaped the neo-scholastic revival, but it is clear throughout that Gilson is concerned with the past only as it sheds light on the present. Once the stage has been set he moves quickly to the main matter at hand.

Identifying his primary targets in leading Thomistic critical realists of his day, Gilson destroys the pretensions of the supposed "realism" of the "I am", of the "I think" and of the "object". Monsignor Noël; Gabriel Picard, Jesuit philosopher at the Jersey scholasticate; M.-D. Roland-Gosselin, the erudite Dominican historian of philosophy and an original thinker in his own right; Joseph Maréchal, the brilliant Jesuit philosopher-psychologist-biologist from Louvain—these men, eminent in their time, are not all widely read today. Nevertheless, their spiritual descendents are numerous[3] and, as Gilson is at pains to point out in the Preface to *Réalisme thomiste*, his critique applies in principle to all critical realisms, no matter what outer clothing the fashion of the day may dictate they wear. This then is no mere tract for the times; the issues involved are of perennial importance to philosophy.

It is instructive to watch Gilson at work, because his tactic, in each case, is to involve his adversary in an internal contradiction in which the critical method devours the realism it is supposed to defend. Granting that it is impossible in practice to refute every attempt at constructing a critical realism (there is no theoretical cutting-off point beyond which men cannot go in this direction), Gilson, by offering his reader a laboratory destruction of the most ambitious attempts at building a critical realism in the early decades of this century, finally confronts the root problem: the theoretical impossibility of reconciling realism with any critical philosophy that would systematically suspend the truth that things are and are in independence of our knowing them. Once the critical starting point is adopted, once our living contact with the world of existing beings is cut, and we start from thought alone, no amount of abstract manipulation of concepts will ever reunite us with the world, no matter how realist our ultimate intentions may be. Whenever the critique gains a foothold within a philosophy, it will invariably eradicate all traces of realism.

[3] We think especially of the many "transcendental Thomisms" which have received so much attention in recent years, even in popular journals. A mark of the continuing importance of *Réalisme thomiste* is that philosophers of this school (Coreth, Lonergan and many more) feel compelled to write, whether implicitly or explicitly, with Gilson's critique in mind.

A foreword ought not to reproduce the text it introduces, but I cannot refrain from indicating, if but briefly, the iron logical structure within which Gilson operates in this book:

> The most representative attempts to reconcile realist metaphysics with idealist presuppositions collapse by the interior fallacies plaguing their own reasoning; any such attempt must fail because two and only two options are open to the philosopher — he takes being as he finds it, and this means he takes himself as he is, the discoverer of an order that antedates himself, or he isolates thought, consciousness, the ego, spirit — however it is called — from the being known by man and from the man who is.

Gilson, who never had much patience with Platonism, is a meat-and-potatoes philosopher for whom the hard solidity of the world was an article of sanity.

If he had stopped at this point, he would still have done contemporary Thomism a great service. But Gilson, although a devastatingly effective critic, could not be content with merely discrediting erroneous positions, and in the last two chapters of *Réalisme thomiste* he proceeds to a positive exposition of true Thomist realism. Starting from the old scholastic saw, *est enim sensus particularium, intellectus vero universalium*, Gilson reveals the foundation of realism in the unity of the knowing subject. This unity of sense and intellect within a knowing subject had been ruptured by the *cogito*; the resulting discontinuity had been accepted by Kant as a *fait accompli*, and his "Copernican Revolution" was little more than a *modus vivendi* designed to "save" the world of Newtonian physics;[4] as we have seen, critical realism's

---

[4] We allude of course to Gilson's brilliant William James lectures at Harvard University, published as *The Unity of Philosophical Experience*.

mistake had been to seek to mend this break while accepting the critical starting point, a self-defeating task. Gilson and other Thomists rediscovered the true solution, to the scandal of the modern world, in the teaching of a thirteenth-century theologian. True, the senses can only grasp particulars and the intellect universals, but sense and intellect are not distinct entities at war with each other. They are powers of a single knowing subject, and through their mutual interpenetration the intellect "sees" the universal in the singular.

Building on this foundation, Gilson, in the final chapter, "The Apprehension of Existence", lays the groundwork for his later studies of existence and judgment. It is here that Gilson approaches the heart of his thirteenth-century master's realism, for he stresses that when man apprehends being he is no longer in the order of essence, *quod quid erat esse*, but of the act of existence. Thus, Thomism transcends the critical problem. Once it is understood that the knowing subject is in direct, living communion with beings that are in act, the supposed problem of bridging the gap between an abstract mind and an equally abstract being is seen in all its poverty, resting in the last analysis on an essentialist notion of being. As we have already noted, in *Being and Some Philosophers* Gilson would follow the course of this impoverished understanding of being through the history of Western philosophy and draw out the consequences for metaphysics and epistemology of St. Thomas' radically *actual* understanding of being.

Etienne Gilson was free of the inferiority complex that plagued so many scholastic philosophers of the time. The dogmatic realism Gilson expounded in *Réalisme thomiste* was not the attitude of a man who closed his eyes to modern philosophy; it was the response of a man who knew that philosophy so intimately that he was convinced that simply understanding it historically was sufficient to know why he did not have to answer it on its own terms. Gilson philosophized, therefore, from a position of strength and not of weakness. It was also the response of a man who was deeply concerned for the future of Thomism. Despite the enormous strides already made in the study of St. Thomas, he saw the future of Thomism threatened by the failure of some of the best minds of the time to understand the unique qualities of the treasure they had inherited and by the desire to gain the plaudits of the modern world by selling that inheritance for a mess of pottage. Unpleasant though the role of a Cassandra might be, his sense of duty would not allow him to remain silent.

Each reader can judge for himself how necessary that warning was and the extent to which it has been heeded. Gilson himself, desirous of healing old wounds opened in the heat of controversy, declined to authorize a translation of *Réalisme thomiste* during his lifetime. The time has now come, however, when this work should be more readily available to the English-speaking community of philosophers. First, of course, because it is still, forty years later, of prime importance in expounding the realist philosophy of St. Thomas. Scarcely less important is the role it played in the development of Gilson's own thought. As we have indicated, *Réalisme thomiste* is the center of Gilson's epistemology, an epistemology which unites his earlier convictions on the reality of Christian philosophy and his later breakthrough to the fecundity of St. Thomas' metaphysics of existence. Finally it remains pivotal to the understanding of current trends in Thomistic epistemology; Gilson penetrated the central issues of Thomistic epistemology so successfully and defined them so clearly that *Réalisme thomiste* has become a touchstone for evaluating all efforts in this field. We have said enough. Let us listen now to a great Christian and a great philosopher.

Frederick D. Wilhelmsen

PREFACE

Le Réalisme méthodique drew the attention of numerous critics, many of whom approached it from differing points of view. Nevertheless, two objections were raised so frequently that I am constrained to see in them the expression of a common attitude worthy of closer consideration. The first objection was that my discussion of critical realism dealt with only two of its proponents, Cardinal Mercier and Monsignor L. Noël. There are certainly others, my critics were quick to point out. Why, they asked, was no mention made of them? *Haec sunt nimium pauca.* The second objection was the contention that by rejecting the critical justification I had transformed the existence of the external world into a simple postulate.[1]

As for the first objection, let me say that I did not see then, and still do not see today, any use in attempting to analyze each individual variety of neo-scholastic critical

[1] "Doesn't it occur to him that if 'the attempt to construct a critical realism is self-contradictory, like the idea of a square circle' (10), realism will be reduced to a pure and simple postulate? And that then there will be nothing left on which to base the perennial philosophy?" U.D.I. in *Angelicum*, 1937, fasc. 3–4, 644. Other critics, whom I must be excused for not citing, have accused me of pragmatism, as if I had not expressly affirmed that realism is based upon the self-evidence of its principles (*Le Réalisme méthodique*, 12). At the time I wrote that book, I never imagined that anyone could confuse a principle with a postulate.

Thomism. A dogmatic discussion is generally exhausted, as far as the essentials go, when one or two examples of the thesis in question have been considered. It is all too easy to set forth the history of a problem at length without deriving any philosophical benefit from doing so. From the names that have been mentioned to me, however, I have become convinced that my critics did not realize the breadth of my conclusions and thus were unable to apply those conclusions to other instances of critical realism. For this reason I feel obliged to renew the discussion and extend my list of critical Thomisms. I am under no illusion that this will appease my adversaries. On the contrary, I realize full well that I will only increase their number. In the first place, no matter how long the list becomes it will still be incomplete, and I will be rebuked for this "failure". Secondly, the discussion of any doctrine must be limited to matter which affords some insight into the precise problem under examination. Otherwise, the essential thread of the argument will be lost amid an infinity of individual instances. Thus, no author can possibly prevent his work from appearing partial and incomplete, at least in the eyes of the persons being discussed and of their partisans. Finally, those whose views have been discussed will not fail to respond. If the author declines to reply to their responses this will be taken as proof of arrogance on his part. If he does reply he will become embroiled in an endless controversy which will cover the same ground time and again without producing any new results. Therefore, let me assure my critics that, although I will do my best to satisfy them, I will surely not be so naive as to think that they *will* be satisfied.

I confess that I was far more surprised at the second objection, and in my eyes it offers the only valid reason for publishing another book on this topic. I never realized just how profoundly classical metaphysics had been contaminated by Kant's *Critique* until a spiritual and intellectual son of St. Thomas Aquinas wrote in a Thomist journal that my position forces me to choose between either a critical realism or a realism reduced to the status of a mere postulate. The Thomism of Thomists who no longer understand the meaning of concepts like "evident" and "human consciousness" is in an advanced state of decay. The present book is therefore a critical analysis of Cartesian-Thomism. In other words, it is an exercise in metaphysical teratology whose principal aim is to deepen our knowledge of healthy metaphysics by a study of pathological forms.

This book is also intended to express my misgivings at the excesses which certain contemporary scholastic circles have indulged in, in the name of philosophical detente. I have said elsewhere that an honest and open disagreement is of more use to philosophy than an illusory reconciliation which masks basic differences. I have been reproached for this "heresy". I will not recant. Philosophy deals with necessities of thought that cannot be compromised. No matter how painful it may be, a dispute is respectable if it is honest. It is impossible to tolerate, in all honesty, the least confusion if one truly believes that the principles of knowledge itself are at stake. In such a case the effort to attain a pure metaphysical position requires a search for formulas free from all taint of compromise. Perhaps I have at times been too extreme in this endeavor. I would have been guilty of this fault far more often had not my text been read and criticized with such care by Mlle. Lucie Gilson, professor of philosophy at the Lycée d'Orléans, whom I must thank for her many useful observations and suggestions.

CHAPTER ONE

REALISM AND COMMON SENSE

After passing twenty centuries as the very model of those self-evident facts that only a madman would ever dream of doubting, the existence of the external world finally received its metaphysical demonstration from Descartes. Yet no sooner had he demonstrated the existence of the external world than his disciples realized that, not only was his proof worthless, but the very principles which made such a demonstration necessary at the same time rendered the attempted proof impossible.

Descartes had first postulated that all self-evident knowledge arises from thought, and from thought alone. From this it follows that the existence of the external world cannot be considered immediately evident, but Descartes hoped to demonstrate the existence of the external world by applying the principle of causality to our sensations. Like everything else, sensations must have a cause. Now, we are not conscious of being their cause; rather, we undergo sensations. Nor are we conscious of receiving them directly from God; on the contrary, we feel that we receive them from beings external to our thought. Since we have no clear and distinct idea that would authorize us to regard God as the cause of our sensations and, on the contrary, have a very strong natural inclination to regard them as caused within us by certain other beings, we must affirm that those beings do exist. For God is perfect and therefore unable to deceive us, but he would be deceiving us if he himself were to give us such ideas directly, all the while allowing us to be controlled by our irresistible natural tendency to believe that sensations come from something outside of us. Therefore, it has been proven that the external world exists.[1]

Thus reduced to its essentials, this demonstration has three main parts. First, an analysis of sensation which makes

[1] See R. Descartes, *Discours de la méthode*, commented upon by E. Gilson (Paris: J. Vrin, 1925), 358–59, concerning moral certitude, which is not, however, an immediate metaphysical proof of the existence of the external world. Concerning the Cartesian demonstration itself, see E. Gilson, *Etudes sur le rôle de la pensée médiévale dans la formation du système cartésien* (Paris: J. Vrin, 1930), 234–35.

It may be worth mentioning here that Descartes himself affirms that his proof of the external world is based upon causality: "It should be noted that this axiom must necessarily be admitted since it alone is the foundation of our knowledge of all things, both sensible as well as those which cannot be grasped by the senses. For how else, for example, do we know that heaven exists?" (Descartes, *Secondes réponses*, ed. Adam Tannery, 9:128). In opposition to this interpretation, which an analysis of the proof itself confirms abundantly, some have tried to maintain that Descartes proves the existence of the external world by means of the divine veracity. This is an obvious distortion which will not suffice to place in doubt the nature of what Descartes did and said that he did. Certainly, divine veracity enters into the proof, but only to prove that the external cause of our sensations is not God. Descartes had foreseen Berkeley and in this way sought to exclude his position. Far from eliminating the proof by causality, the fact of God's veracity actually renders it possible. The divine veracity in effect legitimizes this particular application of the principle of causality, thus permitting him to affirm that the external cause of sensations is indeed the material world of extended bodies.

As for the historical consequences of the Cartesian proof of the existence of the external world, see E. Gilson, *The Unity of Philosophical Experience* (New York: Scribner's, 1937) chap. 2, "The Cartesian Experiment", 125–220.

it appear, in contrast with images, as a fact independent of the will and imposed upon thought from without. Second, an appeal to the principle of causality which permits us to posit, beyond thought, a cause of our sensations. Third, an appeal to the divine veracity to assure us that the true cause of sensations is in fact the existence of created beings distinct from thought, and not God. By proceeding in this manner, Descartes has afforded us a perfect example of a doctrine in which the existence of the external world is arrived at as the result of a deductive proof, using thought itself as a starting point. This is, as was later said, an "illationism", a name which may be applied to any doctrine which proves the existence of the external world by applying the principle of causality to a particular content of thought.[2]

[2] This is why it is impossible to deny that the doctrine of Cardinal Mercier constitutes, on this very point, an illationism of the Cartesian variety (see F. Gilson, *Le Réalisme méthodique* [Paris: Téqui, n d], 18–32). The arguments advanced to distinguish his position from Descartes' are rather curious. It is said that Cardinal Mercier does not base his proof, as did Descartes, upon divine veracity. Nobody claims that he did. Let us say, first of all, with Descartes himself, that the Cartesian proof is based upon the principle of causality, as is Cardinal Mercier's. In order to distinguish the two on this point it would be necessary to prove the contrary. But the most remarkable argument consists of maintaining that Cardinal Mercier merely developed various illationist arguments in passing without incorporating them into his doctrine and, we are assured, without abandoning the immediatism which he had professed from the first. It seems we must choose between making him an immediatist, an illationist or a babbler. I, for one, believe that he was a very coherent illationist. Msgr. L. Noël prefers to maintain, at the same time, the illationism of the Cardinal, which he can hardly deny, and the persistence of his original immediatism, concerning which he adds: "How, then, can we say that his thought is coherent? Here we are reduced to hypotheses, perhaps not entirely satisfactory, which leave us in a certain amount of confusion which it may be impossible entirely to avoid" ("Les Progrès de l'épistémologie thomiste",

Whatever one may think of Descartes' proof, it has this merit: it openly relies upon a deductive process. And it must, since it regards as insufficient our natural feeling that

---

in *Revue néoscolastique de philosophie* 34 [1932]: 430). In other words, he admits to having contradicted himself in order to have one chance in two of being correct. But we need not become involved in such a discussion, for if it is true, and Msgr. Noël assures us it is, that Cardinal Mercier always admitted "a proof of the external world based upon the principle of causality" (art. cit., 431), then the rest of his thought must be interpreted as a function of this constant. This may not be as difficult as we have been told it would be. The texts cited by Msgr. L. Noël (*Notes d'épistémologie thomiste* [Paris and Louvain, 1925], 221–23) are not at all opposed to illationism, for they affirm: 1) the existence of an internal reality, starting point for this illationism; 2) a knowledge of the passivity of our sensations, which will authorize as with Descartes, a search for the cause outside the sensing subject; 3) the fact that the mind, from the outset, represents all that it grasps in nature as existing in itself, which, for Cardinal Mercier, serves to prove that we have a self-evident certitude of the existence of substance. The texts from *Critériologie* cited by Msgr. Noël in "Les progrès de l'épistémologie thomiste" (432, n. 2) present no more problems than the first group of texts. In this group the Cardinal affirms two ideas that he always maintained at the same time and that are not in the least bit contradictory: 1) "We have a direct sensible intuition of external things"; direct, in that we first perceive actual things rather than the fact that we do perceive them; 2) "But it is impossible for us to affirm with certainty the existence of one or many extramental realities without making use of the principle of causality." The basic idea throughout seems to be that the act by which we directly, and without any reflexive intermediary, receive perceptions of the real as real nevertheless does not guarantee any certitude as to the extramental existence of this reality. I must therefore insist that Cardinal Mercier held to a perfectly coherent form of illationism and that he was in agreement with Descartes in that they both considered it necessary to prove the existence of the external world. This could be done by starting from the passive character of sensation and then completing the proof with the aid of the principle of causality. This is the extent of my thesis. It cannot be refuted by disproving what I did not include in it.

the existence of the beings apprehended in virtue of the union of body and soul is self-evident. Instead, it relies upon a special operation of the understanding to confer an intellectual certitude upon our natural feeling, guaranteeing it by means of the principle of causality. The flaw in this doctrine is not in the reasoning itself, which is impeccable, but in the fact that Descartes was unable to explain sensation without admitting the substantial union of body and soul. Now, although Descartes himself did not realize it, such a union is incompatible with his demand for their complete and real distinction. As a result, although they also started with a thought which is thought alone, Regius, Géraud de Cordemoy, Malebranche and, generally speaking, those called "Cartesians" quickly arrived at the conclusion that sensation does not imply any action of the body upon thought.[3] From this it follows that no content of sensation can serve the principle of causality as a starting point from which the existence of the external world may be deduced. Indeed, it was precisely because it was necessary for them to prove the existence of bodies that their proof was impossible. But it mattered little to them. If they could not *prove* that the external world exists, they believed it through faith in revelation. Then came Berkeley, who simply observed that nothing in the Genesis story was changed whether one accepted or denied the existence of matter. He then concluded, and quite logically, that, if it is neither possible to know nor necessary to believe that the external world exists, the wisest thing to say is simply that matter does not exist.[4]

[3] On this subject, see the very clear and well-documented study by H. Gouhier, *La Vocation de Malebranche* (Paris: J. Vrin, 1926), chap. 3, "Le Principe des cartésiens", 80–107.

[4] For a short but more detailed study of this historical problem, see E. Gilson, *The Unity of Philosophical Experience* (New York: Scribner's, 1937), chap. 6, 176–97.

When Thomas Reid recounted this remarkable story[5] he was one of the first to discern its meaning, and it was his intent to escape the magic circle in which philosophers since Descartes had been trapped, mesmerized by the *cogito* and idealism without ever managing to get out. It was in large measure his resolute rejection of the Cartesian approach that led Reid to elaborate his doctrine of "common sense". Reid never pretended that he had discovered common sense, but he tried to give the expression, which itself had become common, a technical philosophical meaning.

For Cicero, common sense was primarily the common manner of feeling, the views of the crowd whose tastes the orator had to take into account if he were to influence them.[6] However, it was also an ensemble of spontaneous judgments with which all men are naturally endowed and which permits them to discern good and evil.[7] This double meaning, commonly accepted opinion and opinion founded upon nature and reason, is almost always found in definitions of common sense. The movement from one meaning to the other is natural and easy. It is not surprising, then, that before Reid, and in a text which Reid himself used, Fénelon had appealed to this spontaneous feeling which guarantees the truth of certain human judgments. "What is common sense?" asks Fénelon.

Nothing but those notions that all men hold concerning the same things. Common sense, which is always and everywhere

[5] Thomas Reid, *Oeuvres complètes*, published by T. Jouffroy (Paris, 1828), 3:148–223; "Essay on the Intellectual Faculties of Man", essay 6, chap. 2: "On Common Sense".

[6] Cicero, *De Oratore*, I, chap. 3 to the end. Cited by J. Lachelier in A. Lalande, *Vocabulaire technique et critique de la philosophie* (Paris: F. Alcan, 1926), 2:75, n. One may find, op. cit., 749–51, other texts of Franck, Jouffroy, etc., on common sense.

[7] Cicero, *De Oratore*, III, chap. 50; cited by T. Reid, op. cit., 39.

the same, which foresees every test, which renders the examination of certain questions ridiculous . . . , this sense which is common to all men, waits only to be consulted, is evident at a glance and discovers in an instant the truth or absurdity of questions; what else could it be but what I call my ideas?[8]

This fund of self-evident knowledge, which Fénelon supported with his doctrine of ideas and which he used to prove the existence of God, was described even more simply by Fr. Buffier in his *Traité des premières vérités et de la source de nos jugements:* "By 'common sense' I understand the disposition given by nature to all men or, manifestly, to the great majority, so that when they have attained the use of reason they may pass common and uniform judgment concerning various objects of private opinion individually perceived. This judgment is not the consequence of any prior principle."[9] For our purposes, the most interesting aspect of Buffier's doctrine of common sense is that he placed it in direct opposition to the Cartesian methodology of the inner sense, and he did so precisely because the Cartesian principle condemns philosophy to solipsism. When you ask the philosophers of the inner sense "if it is self-evident that bodies

[8] Fénelon, *De l'existence de Dieu*, part 2, chap. 2, second proof. Cited by T. Reid, op. cit., 38, and in *Vocabulaire technique et critique de la philosophie*, 2:751.

[9] Buffier, S.J., *Oeuvres philosophique*, ed. Francisque Bouillier (Paris: Charpentier, 1843); *Traité des vérités premières*, part 1, *chap.* 5, 15. In his *Catalogue des Ecrivains du siècle de Louis XIV*, Voltaire says of Fr. Buffier: "There are in his metaphysical treatises certain sections which Locke himself would not have disdained, and he was the only Jesuit whose works contained a reasonable philosophy"; ed. cit., introduction, 1.

One will note that in this passage Buffier begins by distinguishing his conception of common sense from that of the scholastics (op. cit., 14–15). We will return to this point later.

exist and that we receive sensations through the body, they flatly reply: no. . . ."[10] "The first consequence of this principle (of the inner sense) is one we have already touched upon. Since it is not evident that material bodies exist, we cannot be certain that our own bodies exist."[11] Thus, it is against Cartesianism and the idealism which flows from it that Buffier directs his own doctrine of common sense when he cites as the first example of judgments guaranteed by the certainty of common sense: "There are other beings and other men besides myself in the world."[12] So, as far back as 1732, this man, disturbed by the idealist consequences of Cartesianism, could see no other means of avoiding them than by recourse to common sense, that necessary complement to the inner sense, as a guarantee that the external world exists.

Adopted by Reid, then by Jouffroy, Buffier's doctrine could not fail to gain the attention of Catholic theologians, especially when Lamennais espoused it, with modifications, as the foundation for an apologetic of the Christian religion. The danger was obvious. Since common sense was conceived as a sort of sense for the truth, at once infallible yet unjustifiable,

[10] Buffier, *Traité des vérités premières*, part I, chap. 2; ed. cit., 9.

[11] Buffier, op. cit., part I, chap. 3, 10. The text clearly has Malebranche in mind, whom Buffier knew Berkeley followed. Cf. op. cit., part I, chap. 2, n. 15; 9.

[12] Buffier, op. cit., part I, chap. 5, n. 34; 15. T. Reid knew Buffier, whom he cited many times, notably in his *Essays on the Intellectual Faculties*, essay 2, chap. 10, and essay 6, chap. 2. In the latter text Reid speaks of Buffier's writing as "published fifty years ago". The first example of common-sense truths cited by Buffier becomes, in Reid's work, the fifth principle of common sense in the order of contingent truths: "Fifth principle. The objects which we perceive by the agency of the senses really exist, and they are such as we perceive them to be." Op. cit., essay 6, chap. 5; vol. 5, 106.

every attempt to support Christianity by means of this doctrine ran the risk of becoming an irrationalism. Therefore, theologians and Christian philosophers undertook to do what they had attempted so many times: to prevent the spread of an unhealthy idea while recalling its supporters to an acceptable and already received doctrine. Since common sense seemed to so many troubled souls to be an efficacious remedy to skepticism, why not search the traditional philosophy of the schools for the elements of a healthier form of the doctrine of common sense?

Attempts of this kind are not without risk, and although the history of this particular attempt has not yet been written[13] it is not difficult to discern, by means of the internal law which controlled its evolution, the problems that were encountered. At first glance it did not seem impossible to introduce a doctrine of common sense into the economy of Thomism, but the attempt quickly became far more complicated than anyone had imagined it would be. In the first place, nothing called common sense can be found in St. Thomas except for a psychological thesis with no bearing

[13] Such a history would not be entirely useless. It would have to take account not only of Liberatore's work, whose position we have analyzed, but also of Sanseverino's *Institutiones seu elementa philosophiae christianae cum antiqua et nova comparatae*, the fourth volume of which (*Theologia naturalis*) appeared in 1870. Cf. "Concerning Common Sense", in the edition of Signoriello (Naples, 1885); 1:626–30.

T. M. Zigliara, *Summa philosophica in usum scholarium* (Rome, 1876). Cf. 8th ed. (Lyon and Paris, 1891), 1:257–59 and 277–81. Also see p. 279 of Sanseverino's *I principali sistemi della Filosofia sul Criterio*, cap. 3, 2.

One will note the effort which these authors made to eliminate from their notion of common sense any implications of irrationality such as are found in Reid. The example of Reid seems to have led them to give common sense, as understood by Cicero and Seneca, a more important and more explicitly defined status than that which it had in classical scholasticism.

on the question at hand. In his commentary on the *De Anima* of Aristotle, St. Thomas defines common sense according to the strictest letter of the peripatetics: "Sensus enim communis est quaedam potentia, ad quam terminantur immutationes omnium sensuum".[14] Four centuries later Bossuet faithfully restated this definition: "This faculty of the soul which organizes sense impressions . . . so that one unified object is formed from everything received by the senses is called common sense. This term is sometimes transferred to the operations of the intellect, but its proper meaning is the one we have just pointed out."[15] Truth to tell, there had been no transfer of the term; it was simply that *sensus* can signify both "sense" and "sensation". It was impossible to translate κοινὴ αἴσθησις other than by *sensus communis*, just as it was impossible to translate the *sensus communis* of Cicero and Seneca other than by "common sense". It was simply a case of equivocation, and Bossuet, who knew the two possible meanings, did not hesitate to maintain that the proper meaning was the first.

Nevertheless, this equivocation was an open invitation to look for a passage whose meaning fell somewhere between the psychology of Aristotle and the rhetoric of Cicero. The κοιναὶ δόξαι of Aristotle satisfied the need. "I call the principles of demonstration," says Aristotle, "which serve as the basis for all proofs, common beliefs [τὰς κοινὰς δόξας], such as: everything must of necessity be either affirmed or denied, and: it is impossible for anything to both exist and not exist at the same time, as well as all other premises of this kind."[16] The meaning of this text is clear.

[14] St. Thomas Aquinas, *De Anima*, bk. 2, lect. 13; Pirotta ed., n. 390. Cf. bk. 3, lect. 3; ed. cit., nn. 610–13.

[15] Bossuet, *Traité de la connaissance de Dieu et de soimême,* ed. L. Rossigneux (Paris: Lecaffre, 1900), chap. 1, n. 4, 46.

[16] Aristotle, *Metaphysics*, B, II, 996b 27–31.

As St. Thomas observed, Aristotle is simply saying that every proof presupposes certain evident principles which are themselves indemonstrable. These *dignitates*, or axioms, are naturally and immediately known by all men, thus the name κοιναὶ δόξαι; "et quia talis cognitio principiorum inest nobis statim a natura, concludit [Aristotle], quod omnes artes et scientiae, quae sunt de quibusdam aliis cognitionibus, utuntur praedictis principiis tanquam naturaliter notis."[17] This is the ensemble of "common conceptions"

[17] St. Thomas Aquinas, *In Metaphysics*, bk. 3, lect. 5; Cathala edition, n. 389. It is necessary to add to these principles their obvious implications. Thus, "communis conceptio dicitur illa cujus oppositum contradictionem includit; sicut omne totum est major sua parte . . . "; but also: "naturam animae rationalis non esse corruptibilem, haec est communis animi conceptio" (*De Potentia* q. 5, a. 3, ad 7). Thus, the Thomist idea of *communes conceptiones* is flexible. One may first distinguish here, with Boethius (*De Hebdomadibus*, init.), two kinds of common ideas: those that are known by everyone and those that are known only by the learned. Therefore, each instance must be examined separately. Everything the opposite of which is contradictory is *res per se nota* and *communis conceptio* both for the many and for the learned, but there are degrees of certitude for truths of this sort. For example: *ex nihilo nihil fit* was considered a *communis conceptio* by Aristotle; and it is, but only in the order of secondary causes, for an exception must be made in the case of creation (*Summa Theologica*, I, q. 45, a. 2. ad 1: *De Potentia, q.* 3, a. 1, ad 1). The existence of God is not *res per se nota*, and St. Thomas neither affirms nor denies that it is a *communis conceptio* in the technical sense; he merely says that we have an innate knowledge of this truth in the sense that all men have the ability to arrive at it (*De Veritate*, 10, 12, Resp. and ad 1). If you apply the strict Thomistic definition from the commentary on the *De Hebdomadibus*, cap. 1: "communis animi conceptio, vel principium per se notum, (est) aliqua propositio ex hoc quod praedicatum est de ratione subjecti" (ed. Mandonnet, 1:170), it seems hard to say that the existence of God could be, in this sense a *communis conceptio*, at least as far as we are concerned. In the case of natural law St. Thomas explains in great detail the difference between the community of principles and the conclusions drawn from them, according to whether we are dealing

understood in the Thomist sense which Lamennais' adversaries decided to call "common sense".

Thus understood, the common sense of the neo-scholastics became, from around the beginning of the nineteenth century, something entirely different from that of Lamennais or Reid. Liberatore was too good a Thomist not to be fully aware of the real nature of the work he had accomplished, and Sanseverino and Zigliara were not inferior to him in that respect. For them, common sense, as understood by their adversaries, remained an *opinatio quaedam rejicienda*[18] which had been combined with the doctrine of Reid. They therefore rejected this badly defined innate faculty, concerning which all that was known was that it promulgated infallibly true judgments, although these judgments were neither immediately self-evident nor founded upon experience nor were conclusions of a process of reasoning. In reality, the apologetics of common sense attempted to restore Reidianism — *Reidianum commentum restaurat* — that is, it attempted to base the whole edifice of true knowledge upon instinctive and, therefore, irrational judgments. Nothing, says Liberatore, is more pernicious than such a doctrine, nothing more contrary to reason. For if thought is unable to reject these judgments, although they are neither evident nor demonstrated, it will have to

---

with the speculative or practical realm (*Summa Theologica*, I, II, q. 94, a. 4, Resp.). Here it is clear that once we leave the realm of principles the status of a *communis conceptio* is extremely variable, depending upon the degree of removal from the principles and the aptitude of the individual reason to grasp their consequences. No text has ever come to our knowledge in which St. Thomas considers these common conceptions to be the product of some *sensus communis*.

[18] Matt. Liberatore, *Institutiones philosophicae*; prima editio novae formae, Log. pars 2, cap. 3 "De Veritatis criterio" a. 6; Prato, 1881; 1:163–64. Cf. Zigliara, *Summa Philosophica*, ed. 8, 1:284–86.

submit to certitudes which are at once in conformity with reason, inasmuch as reason does accept them, yet irrational, since they cannot be justified: all of which is contradictory and impossible. In fact, although invented as a remedy to skepticism, common sense thus conceived is quite at home with it. It has landed us upon the very rock from which it was meant to save us.

Thus far Liberatore's position is beyond reproach; but it is more difficult for Thomists to say what common sense *is* than to say what it is not. When common sense is reduced to the *communes sententias* of St. Thomas, two problems inevitably arise: the first concerns the nature of common sense, and the second concerns its content. First, its nature. Is it a new faculty attributable to reason? Or is it reason itself exercising its spontaneous and natural function? As long as you are content to speak of *communes conceptiones animi*, as St. Thomas was, the problem does not arise, since these "common conceptions" are simply judgments formulated by reason in the light of the principle of contradiction. But the problem does arise when the ensemble of these judgments is attributed to a vague *sensus communis*. Hence the marked hesitation by Liberatore in his definition of common sense: "[*Vis illa*] a natura rationali proveniens, seu ipsa ratio naturalis, prout sponte sua in ejusmodi judicia prorumpit, appelatur sensus communis."[19] No formula could be better balanced, but it would be nice to know if this new common sense is a faculty of reason or is reason itself. Liberatore carefully avoids telling us, for if common sense is *not* reason itself we fall into Reid's irrationalism once again; but if it *is* reason itself it will not serve as a replacement for that instinct for the truth with which he sought to oppose

[19] Liberatore, op. cit., 1:162.

skepticism. If it is to be more than just a word, it must be something: something adapted to carrying out the specific function it was developed to perform.

Liberatore's indecision can be still better understood if we ask just what the content of this new common sense is. A good Thomist, Liberatore begins by defining the truths of common sense as *judicia haec quae Aristoteles communes sententias appellavit*. This was both wise and legitimate, but his decision obliged him to limit the list of the truths of common sense to the *communes conceptiones animi* of St. Thomas, that is, those facts which are self-evident in light of the principle of contradiction and its immediate applications. Certainly there was nothing to prevent him from limiting the truths of common sense in this manner; in fact, his definition actually invited such a procedure, but the doctrine of common sense would then have become as useless for him as it was for St. Thomas. If the *sensus communis* had been reduced to the self-evidence of principles, it would not have been able to guarantee those truths which Liberatore wanted it to. The truths he had in mind were actually those which Cicero, Seneca and Plutarch had used common sense to justify, rather than the κοιναὶ δόξαι of Aristotle and St. Thomas. Briefly, what was needed was to extend the self-evidence of the metaphysical *communes conceptiones* to the *sensus communis* of rhetoric. It was necessary to expand the first until it included the second and to consolidate the second while absorbing it into the first. I do not want to say that this is impossible, but it is not easy; and Liberatore seems to have finally come up short in the attempt.

Let us consider his examples of the truths of common sense. Along with genuine *communes conceptiones* are found others of much more doubtful origin: bodies exist; God exists; the human soul survives the body; the good will be rewarded and the evil punished in a future life; and others of this sort.[20] In these statements Liberatore sees so many conclusions of natural reason, distinguishable from philosophical conclusions in only two respects. In the first place, they do not belong to any particular individual but to the whole human race. Secondly, they are spontaneous conclusions, not products of conscious reflection: "Sine artis praesidio et sola vi naturalis ingenii".[21] I will certainly not deny the existence or the widespread acceptance of these spontaneous convictions, nor will I contest either their rhetorical and persuasive value or the considerable importance which their existence holds for philosophy.[22] The general characteristics of these

[20] Ibid.

[21] Ibid., 164.

[22] The most sustained effort to integrate a doctrine of common sense into Thomism is that of Fr. Réginald Garrigou-Lagrange, *Le Sens commun, la philosophie de l'être et les formules dogmatiques* (Paris: Nouvelles Librairie National), 81–87. For him common sense *is* philosophy, the *perennis quaedam philosophia* Leibniz speaks of, but in a rudimentary state (84). Therefore, he proposes a "conceptualist-realist theory of common sense: which, it seems, can easily be drawn out of the writings of Aristotle or of the great scholastics" (85). Naturally, Fr. Garrigou-Lagrange is unable to find a single text from Aristotle or the great scholastics to cite in favor of common sense. When he says that it "reappears" in Fénelon, he neglects to mention where it had previously appeared as a philosophical doctrine. Except for Fénelon, he—like everyone else—can only cite Reid and Jouffroy, after which he calmly concludes: "The scholastics expressed themselves in the same manner" (87). Who are these scholastics? The only one he cites is Cardinal Zigliara (*Summa Philosophica*, 1:257). The same question arises once more. Why, if realism had always been critical, did the scholastics fail to realize this until after they had read Kant, or why, if their philosophy had always been *the* philosophy of common sense, did the scholastics fail to realize it until after they had read Reid? If "common sense" is truly a distinct faculty, why not show us what role it plays in the Thomistic description of the knowing subject. If it is merely a "quality common to all men, equal in all and

certitudes are their relative universality, their stability and their persistence.[23] I would not even care to deny that, as the happy expression of Seneca has it, the belief of all men is an indication of or an argument for the truth.[24] The real difficulty begins when the attempt is made to assimilate such beliefs into the "common opinions" of classic scholasticism and place them on an equal plane as regards their nature and certainty.

If the certitudes of common sense are, according to Liberatore's definition, *judicia haec quae Aristoteles communes sententias appellavit*, it is necessary to attribute to this formula the same narrow meaning that Aristotle himself gives it. And if this is done, it immediately becomes necessary to make at least one important exception to the universal belief in the immortality of the soul as well as to the belief in a

---

invariable" (87), common sense begins to break down into its constituent parts: on the one hand, first principles of the intellect and spontaneous judgments of speculative or practical reason (which are sufficiently explained by the intellect and reason without any need for recourse to a new and distinct faculty), on the other hand, confused social opinions and prejudices which rational reflection will expose as pseudocertitudes, which no "common sense" has the right to uphold against reason. The particular "quality" which is invoked to explain the generality of the contents of common sense points out nothing more than the essential universality of intellect and reason. It is impossible to introduce "common sense" into the Thomist synthesis without introducing a dose, no matter how infinitesimal, of Reid, and thus sowing the seeds of its destruction. Unless, of course, it is only introduced as a formula devoid of all content in order to clothe the *perennis philosophia* in the passing fashion of the day, which offers nothing of philosophical interest. When Bergson defines the philosophy of Plato and Aristotle as "the natural metaphysics of the human intellect", he speaks as a true philosopher. This is a profound formula which does not make natural metaphysics into a "common sense".

[23] Liberatore, op. cit., 1:162.

[24] Seneca, *ad Lucil.*, epist. 117; cited by Liberatore, 1:162, n. 1.

future life of rewards and punishments. Although he learned about these doctrines from his master Plato, Aristotle says nothing to us about them, and nothing entitles us to suppose that he numbered them among "those common opinions which serve as the basis for all demonstration". Among such "common opinions" of Aristotle as: everything must necessarily be either affirmed or denied, or: it is impossible for something to both be and not be at the same time, the further proposition that the good will be rewarded and the evil punished in a future life would be totally out of place. To be sure, all these formulas are rational, but not all in the same way. It is simply arbitrary legislation to group, under one "common sense", both the knowledge of those principles whose self-evidence governs all certitude and the obscure anticipations of reason which seize upon the truth without actually seeing it. But there is more. If the certitudes of common sense are identified with the *communes conceptiones* of St. Thomas, can we consider "God exists" to be one of them? This presents, at the very least, a serious difficulty. In his commentary on the *De Hebdomadibus* St. Thomas defines what he calls *communis animi conceptio vel principium per se notum* as a proposition in which *praedicatum est de ratione subjecti*. Now, everyone knows that according to St. Thomas the existence of God is not a proposition known *per se quoad nos*. If every common conception is a principle known *per se*, or can be immediately reduced thereto, the existence of God cannot be a common conception. If, therefore, the truths of common sense are identified with the common conceptions of St. Thomas, "God exists" is not a truth of common sense. St. Thomas would probably reject such a conclusion if he were alive today, but not without noting that the *sensus communis* of Cicero and Seneca cannot be likened to the common conceptions, at least not as he and Aristotle understood them. Every common conception is part of common sense, but everything which is part of common sense is not necessarily a common conception. Common sense, such as Liberatore had conceived it, was therefore an equivocal notion whose inherent contradictions presented numerous difficulties to his successors.

Like so many before and after him, Liberatore had allowed himself to be seduced by the promise of aid which his misguided efforts seemed to offer to classical metaphysics. Endeavors of this sort always end in defeat. In order to confer a technical philosophical value upon the common sense of orators and moralists it is necessary either to accept Reid's common sense as a sort of unjustified and unjustifiable instinct, which will destroy Thomism, or to reduce it to the Thomist intellect and reason, which will result in its being suppressed as a specifically distinct faculty of knowledge. In short, there can be no middle ground between Reid and St. Thomas.

Because they believed that there *was* such a middle ground, Liberatore and his successors introduced a foreign body into the structure of Thomist epistemology, and its presence is still considered a threat. To equate the obscure certitudes of common sense with the common conceptions and, at the same time, confer upon common sense the self-evidence of the latter was to introduce the most far-reaching and deplorable tendencies into philosophy. From this moment on many authors of philosophical treatises gave in to the temptation of defending the fundamental verities of Thomism by crushing their opponents under the weight of common sense, which had only to be affirmed to be justified. Was the existence of the external world in question? Bodies exist, replied Liberatore's common sense, and *voilà*, the matter was settled, as if Malebranche had not considered a proof of their existence to be impossible and Berkeley denied their existence in the name of common sense itself. The most serious problem with such a method was that by calling this false friend to the aid of metaphysical certitude the impression was given that metaphysical certitude could not do without common sense. Common sense was a poor ally, a cause of weakness to the philosophy which attempted to establish a firm foundation upon it, and its inadequacies became apparent when those who relied upon it tried to use it to prove the existence of the external world. They began by affirming it as a truth of common sense, then undertook to justify this certitude itself and, almost without realizing it, yielded to the very idealism which they had intended to refute.

The criteriology of Sebastian Reinstadler, whose manual represented the purest Thomism for generations of professors and students,[25] is a remarkable witness to the ravages caused by this method. From the moment the problem of idealism is mentioned there can be no doubt concerning this author's position nor the ease with which he will vindicate it, for he defines idealism as an error, which makes its refutation much simpler. "Idealism", writes Reinstadler, "is the error of those who, rejecting the trustworthiness of the senses and the common sense of all, deny or cast doubt upon the existence of bodies."[26] The refutation of Berkeley and Fichte presents no problem to this champion of common sense, for their positions contradict common sense: "In idealismo refutando non est cur tempus teramus: ejus enim doctrina sensui communi tam aperte contradicit, ut nemo sit, qui absurditates ejus facile non detegat."[27] Against

---

[25] Sebastian Reinstadler, *Elementa philosophiae scholasticae* (Freiburg im Breisgau, 1904). The description of common sense as *testimonium doctrinale* of the truth is found in his *Criteriologia*, vol. 1, cf. the *Elementa*, 198–99.

[26] Reinstadler, op. cit., 1:172.

[27] Ibid., 174.

Fichte it will suffice to invoke the testimony of the inner sense, which assures us of the passive character of our sensations. As for Berkeley, it is evident that our sensations come to us through our sense organs and that they are not produced in us immediately by God. These two arguments would have carried weight if Fichte and Berkeley had not already conceded both of them, for Fichte searched at length in the ego for the opposition which the ego creates, and Berkeley took care to establish that our sense organs are themselves ideas. Moreover, these arguments fail to reach the heart of the matter, for if you wish to argue on the basis of common sense it will be necessary to first ask why, since common sense is universal by definition, Berkeley and Fichte were the only two men deprived of it. And after that question has been answered we must also explain why their lack of common sense has given philosophers so much food for thought. What is most remarkable, however, is that, despite the offhand manner in which Reinstadler treats this question, his common sense itself does not escape unscathed.

For it too is subject to the law which requires that every refutation of an error founded upon the consequences of that very error must inevitably fall back into the same error from whose consequences it took its starting point. This can be seen quite clearly in the arguments marshalled by Reinstadler against idealism, for, although said to be drawn from the purest common sense, in fact they reproduce the exact arguments by which Cartesian idealism tried to avoid its own proper consequences: "Experimur enim nos sensationes saepe habere, quando nolumus, non habere et contra saepe, quando maxime eas volumus." This is one of the principal supports of the Cartesian proof of the external world, and it enjoys a remarkable popularity in contemporary neo-scholasticism.[28] Of course this argument proves nothing, since the facts are explained equally well by Berkeley's thesis that our ideas are the language the Author of nature speaks to man. Even before Berkeley, Malebranche had already noted that if one accepts occasionalism and the vision of God which results from it, the existence or nonexistence of the external world is a matter of indifference as far as the content of our thought is concerned. If our sensations come to us from God, they are as independent of our will as if they came from an external world of bodies. This is why Descartes, foreseeing the possibility of an absolute idealism, had completed his proof by adding that a God who himself causes our sensations while allowing us to believe that they were caused by an external world of bodies would be a deceitful and therefore imperfect God, a contradictory and impossible concept.

One can but marvel at the docility with which Reinstadler and other scholastics followed Descartes down this blind alley: "De actione Dei immediata in nobis nihil omnino conscientia refert", and: "Repugnat enim Deum, veritatis amantem et infinitate bonum, creaturam suam rationalem in errore invincibili his in terris perpetuo velle detinere."[29] Whatever the intrinsic merit of this argument,

---

[28] A detailed comparison of Descartes' and Cardinal Mercier's texts can be found in *Le Réalisme méthodique*, 18–32. The argument seems to have been popularized among modern scholastics by J. Balmes, *La Philosophie fondamentale*, bk. 2, chap. 5. However, Balmes was uneasy as to the possible consequences of his attitude, as can be seen from the beginning of chap. 6. In contrast, the argument was adopted without hesitation by J. S. Hickey, *Summula philosophiae scholasticae,* 4th ed., (Dublin, 1915); 1:212. For Reinstadler's text, which we have just cited, see the following note.

[29] Reinstadler, 174–75. The author refers, for further information on this point, to Frick, *Logica*, 190ff., and to Mercier, *Critériologie générale*, 352ff. Cf. J. S. Hickey, *Summula philosophiae scholasticae*, loc. cit.

it is easy to see why Descartes used it, for he had proven the existence of God before the existence of the external world. God is able to guarantee the external world in a philosophy that uses the idealist method, but it is truly surprising that a scholastic realist for whom the existence of God is proven by means of the external world should, at the same time, undertake to prove the existence of the world by means of the existence of God. Such an attitude is not even eclecticism: it is sheer intellectual chaos.

How could they fail to see the results of such a method? If it is truly divine veracity that guarantees the reliability of our sensations, the existence of the external world is no longer self-evidently certain and can in turn only be guaranteed by the existence of God. But then how can God's existence be proven from the existence of the external world, since before being sure that there is an external world we must first be sure that God exists? There is no escape from this dead end. Whoever sticks a finger into the machinery of the Cartesian method must expect to be dragged along its whole course. For, after all, as soon as the problem of the existence of the external world was presented in terms of common sense, Cartesianism was accepted. Descartes never denied that the existence of the external world was a common-sense truth. On the contrary, he expressly affirmed that it was, positing this truth as a moral certitude that for the most part suffices for the needs of life.

Only a hyperbolic doubt would ever question it. The problem was to transform this common-sense certitude into a metaphysical certitude. This is why, forced by his method to deny that the existence of the external world is evident, he had to undertake its proof. To reduce realism to the level of common sense is to reduce it to the status of infraphilosophic knowledge, and this is what Descartes did first. He then borrowed its arguments to free himself from the impasse in which he found himself. Now, nothing prevented the realist Reinstadler from holding that the existence of the external world is self-evident. Descartes had been mistaken in this matter, but he, at least, had been philosophically mistaken and sank in his own ship, whereas Reinstadler sank with him but in a ship which was not his own and upon which he had no right to embark.

Perhaps some might be surprised that we attach so much importance to the fact that the contradictory nature of these attempts dooms them to failure. The reason we do is because, although devoid of any philosophic value, they are in a certain measure responsible for much of the contemporary controversy concerning the possibility of critical realism. By the very scorn which it inspired in the better interpreters of Aristotelian realism, common-sense realism sent them in the opposite direction; or rather, since they were deceived as to principles, their horror at this pseudophilosophy induced them to invent false classifications for which there was no need.[30] If ever there was a naive realism, common-sense

[30] This preoccupation is evident, for example, in Msgr. L. Noël, "L'Epistemologie thomiste", in *Acta secundi congressus thomistici internationalis* (Taurini-Romae: Marietti, 1937). There, Msgr. Noël opposes certain adversaries whom he leaves unnamed, but he tells us that these "excellent minds" contest "the necessity and even the legitimacy of epistemology" which, in their eyes, is a useless exercise foreign to the thought of Aristotle and St. Thomas, and even "necessarily ruinous" (32). I admit that I do not know who maintained such a position, and I regret that I do not know who it was who said that it is necessary "to reject all epistemology, to extricate ourselves from the 'problem of knowledge', which is nothing but a false problem, and to renounce any intention of attempting a rapprochement between the scholastic and modern points of view, which can only result in confusion; rather, we should point out their honest differences so that clarity may result" (32). The problem is, having only recently used the expression "honest

realism was it. In reaction to it, these philosophers announced that they intended to adopt a philosophical attitude in these matters. Their realism was therefore styled "critical realism", as opposed to the naive realism of common sense.[31] That is all the more clearsighted among them

---

disagreement" (*Le Réalisme méthodique*, 82), I must ask, with some uneasiness, am I the one in question here? The least reference to the authors responsible for these positions would have reassured me. Whatever the truth of the matter may be, I must be permitted to reiterate that the disagreement between Msgr. Noël and myself has nothing to do with a denial of the legitimacy or necessity of epistemology but with the method which he follows in his epistemology. I cannot accept Msgr. Noël's position that epistemology has priority in relation to metaphysics or, as he would say, that "the ontological theory of knowledge is logically posterior to epistemology" (art. cit., 58. Cf. 45, art. 1). What I am asking for is a realist epistemology within metaphysics. If Msgr. Noël objects, "It is hard to see what could be put in place of epistemology, and certainly there must be something with which to oppose idealism" (32), I will simply reply that the conflict is not between realism and epistemology but between realist epistemology and idealist epistemology. True, we need something with which to oppose idealism, and that something is realism.

[31] "Immediate realism is inevitable because it is an obvious fact beyond which it is impossible to proceed further. This does not mean, however, that Thomist realism should be a naive realism; on the contrary, it is a realism which is perfectly well aware of its basis in reason, and that is why it truly deserves the name 'critical'." (R. Jolivet, *Le Thomisme et la critique de la connaissance* [Paris: Desclée de Brouwer, 1933], 111). Thus, immediate realism is a *self-evident fact based upon reason* and therefore is an *immediately critical fact*. Even if we were to resign ourselves to using this bizarre terminology, we would still have to ask why the reasons which form the basis of this self-evident fact are couched by preference in terms of a "critical doubt" (117), a "realist *cogito*" (91) and a "realist critique" (30). It would seem that "critical realism" is just another name "generally applied to Thomism" (29). But since when has this been so? Can the expression be traced back beyond Kant? Or should

wanted to say,[32] and it must be admitted that they said it, but it would have been better to have said it differently.

This mode of expression supposes that "critical" and "naive" are opposites, as if whatever is not naive has the right to be called critical. At this rate all philosophy would be critical by definition, since all philosophy involves reflection. Certainly it is possible to take that position, but it is unnecessary to express oneself in that way. Moreover, such language involves many drawbacks. It is unnecessary, for if it is true that the mode of knowledge proper to common sense is infraphilosophic, naive realism cannot be elevated to the level of philosophy. Therefore, there is no reason to use

---

we say that Thomism performed the critique of knowledge for centuries, just as M. Jourdain wrote prose, without knowing it? To avoid making Thomism into a naive realism it has been transformed into a naive criticism which was unaware of what it was doing until it donned its new Kantian clothing. This is hardly progress.

[32] This is what the following lines of Msgr. Noël suggest: "They [the ancients] did not hesitate to affirm common sense realism as a postulate; they had thought out the fundamentals of the position, although still only in a rough outline. . . ." Art. cit., 32. As for the above, it should be noted: 1) that to posit the existence of the external world as self-evident for man is not the same as regarding it as a postulate. A postulate is not self-evident; what is self-evident is not postulated, it is seen. 2) It should also be observed that Msgr. Noël's formula simply equates reflective knowledge and critical knowledge; if this were true, critical realism would be the same as philosophical realism, and there would be no point in even using the word "critical". The same remark applies to those excellent pages devoted by J. Maritain to the reconciliation of philosophy and common sense (Eléments de philosophie, 6th ed. [Paris, 1921], 87–94). I can think of nothing to add to what he has said; it clearly appears that for J. Maritain philosophical knowledge requires a reflection upon the givens of common sense, which is what the critic does (90; 3, a; cf. 91; b, 2) and also what the philosopher does. Thus, it is easy to see why J. Maritain insists upon using the term "critical realism" (Les Degrés du savoir [Paris: Desclée, 1932], 137–58). He concludes by asking: "After these

the expression, as if it were necessary to distinguish, outside of philosophy, between a realism that is naive and one that is not. If it is naive, realism is simply not philosophy; if it is philosophy, realism cannot be naive. Aside from the fact that neither Aristotle nor St. Thomas did, we need not style ourselves critical realists for the simple fact that we are realists of the reflective sort, which is the manner of philosophy itself. So let us say that we hold a philosophical realism and, since the problem only arises among philosophers, content ourselves with calling it realism, plain and simple.

For not only is there no need to use the expression "critical realism", it also presents serious drawbacks. If it were merely a matter of protecting Kant's rights to the word "critical", we would hardly take the trouble. The word belongs to everyday speech in its usual sense of "to judge". Therefore, all philosophy has the right to use it, even in a philosophical sense, provided only that a distinct meaning corresponds to the use to which it is put. This is what Kant did when he decided to call his idealism "critical", as opposed to all other

---

explanations, will M. Gilson finally be convinced that the objections against the possibility of a critical Thomism are not insurmountable, and that the concept of a critical realism is not self-contradictory, like the concept of a square circle?" (156). To which I simply reply that if critical knowledge is the same as philosophical knowledge, a philosopher who defends any epistemology does it as a critical philosopher, but the word "critical" adds nothing to the concept of philosophy. So it is true that within the philosophical order the expression "critical realism" will either lose all distinct meaning (in which case it will not be self-contradictory), or else it will signify a certain manner of posing the problem, which consists of admitting that realism can be a postulate but denying that it is immediately self-evident. The general thesis of the present work is that as soon as "critical realism" acquires a distinct meaning it becomes self-contradictory.

forms of idealism and, consequently, of philosophy. If a realist intends to reclaim the title for his own doctrine or wants to use this term to signify that his realism is conscious of its foundations, justified by reflection rather than the spontaneous certitude of common sense, either "critical realism" will simply mean "philosophical realism" or else "critical" will acquire a meaning distinct from "philosophical". In the latter case, experience shows and reason proves that it will become necessary to justify realist conclusions with the help of an idealist method. It is precisely this question, whether the latter approach is intrinsically possible, that we must examine.

CHAPTER TWO

IMMEDIATE REALISM AND THE
CRITIQUE OF KNOWLEDGE

It is rather remarkable that of all the realisms which claim the right to the title "critical" immediate realism should do so the most vigorously: remarkable, because, if the compatibility of realism and criticism could be proven in such an extreme case, it would seem certain beyond a doubt that the two are not irreconcilable. We ought, therefore, to examine this question first of all: is it possible for a realism to be both immediate and critical at the same time?

The expression "immediate realism" is clear on its face. It includes every realism which holds that the mind is able to grasp immediately a reality independent both of the thought which represents it and of the act of thought which apprehends it.[1] The meaning of the word "critical" is much less clear. It is here, as we shall see, that the confusion begins. However, since immediate critical realism offers its own definition, we should examine that first. According to this school the proper object of a "critical" justification of realism is "to satisfy the requirement laid down by modern thought since Descartes which seeks to ground philosophy upon an indisputable certainty".[2] The words "laid down"

[1] For a detailed exposition of immediate realism, see L. Noël, *Notes d'épistémologie thomiste* (Louvain and Paris, 1925). For a discussion of this doctrine, see E. Gilson, *Le Réalisme méthodique* (Paris: Téqui, n.d.), 32–44.

[2] L. Noël, "La Méthode du réalisme" in *Revue néoscolastique de*

(*prononcée*) may seem too strong at first, but they were not chosen at random. Although the supporters of this type of realism claim that this requirement dates back earlier than Descartes, we shall see that it gained much wider acceptance after the publication of the *Discourse on Method* and today, thanks to Descartes' influence, is more strictly enforced than ever.

We may accept this definition provisionally, but we must still ask: what does it really mean? To maintain that a philosophy receives its critical justification when it has been firmly grounded upon some indisputable starting point could mean one of two different things. It could mean either that the critical justification is an integral part in the actual formation of the philosophy or that it is applied to the philosophy after it has already been constructed. The strict letter of the formula rather suggests the second alternative, but we must examine both, since the first is still possible and also because they both present certain difficulties.

If by "critical justification of realism" we are to understand an operation by which realism is grounded upon some indisputable starting point, we can easily see why, and with reference to what, such a viewpoint claims the title "critical". We have just challenged the existence of infra-philosophic realisms, common-sense realisms, and we have

---

philosophie (1931): 437. At the beginning of this article (433) is a bibliography of studies by Msgr. Noël on this subject. Add to that list: L. Noël, "Réalisme méthodique ou réalisme critique", in *Bulletins de la classe des Lettres . . . de L'Acad. royal de Belgique,* 5th series, 17 (1931): III–29. "Les Progrès de l'épistémologie thomiste", in *Revue néoscolastique de philosophie* (1932) 432–48. "L'Épistémologie thomiste", in *Acta secundi congressus thomistici internationalis* (Taurini-Romae: Marietti, 1937), 31–42. Several of these studies have since been collected in L. Noël, *Le Réalisme immédiat* (Louvain, 1938).

noted their pretensions to play a role in philosophy. It is readily understandable that realists faithful to the traditions of St. Thomas and Aristotle would prefer not to be seen in such company, although if it came to making a choice between common sense and Kant, they would certainly choose common sense. In fact, many of them have chosen it. Yet in a certain sense these realists feel more comfortable with Kant for, although idealism may be false, it is at least a philosophy, whereas common sense is not. Therefore, when these realists refer to their philosophy as "critical", they wish above all to indicate that their realism is truly a philosophy, one which has attained an explicit, conscious grasp of a starting point whose validity none may contest.

We have already noted this concern in the claims which certain contemporary realists make to the title "critical". This explains why these realists find it so difficult to distinguish between a non-critical realism and a naive common-sense realism,[3] as if pre-critical or non-critical thought were necessarily "naive". However, explaining the origin of an expression does not justify its use. If it is true that in the case outlined above the word "critical" merely means "philosophical", it is tautological to say that a realist philosophy is critical. Taken in itself the word "critical" has no distinct meaning in such a statement; properly speaking it is meaningless.

Perhaps it may be objected that it is quite proper to use a distinct term, "critique", to designate a distinct operation: that by which a philosophy bases itself upon an incontestable starting point. This objection would be valid if the critique could be conceived of as a distinct operation that

---

[3] "It can be seen that methodic realism differs from naive realism only in its historic situation and in the conscious decision from which it arose" (L. Noël, "La Méthode du réalisme", 436).

makes a philosophy truly a philosophy, but that is impossible. A philosophy that is not based upon indisputable principles is not fully constituted as a philosophy. If a philosophy is to be truly deserving of the name, it must be based upon the science of first causes and principles: metaphysics. Thus, the operation by which realism is able to discredit common sense's attempt to elevate itself to the status of philosophy is simply the same as that by which realism is related to the first principles of metaphysics. Therefore, such a realism will be critical not only to the extent that it is philosophical but also to the extent that it is metaphysical. Thus, we are once more confronted with the intrinsic impossibility of the preceding position. Such a formula strips the word "critical" of all distinct meaning.

The partisans of critical realism are fully aware of the weight of these objections, and we will later see those partisans striving to give a satisfactory answer to them. Since these realists define their viewpoint as critical, they must prove that their critique adds something extra to what other philosophers call philosophy. As a result they feel constrained to adopt, in a very literal sense, the definition with which we began this discussion. Therefore, to base philosophy upon an indisputable starting point will mean to search for a privileged proof, perhaps unique, which will confirm our philosophical certitudes by means of a special operation—the critique. This time we have a definite content for the word "critical", but we must now ask whether the philosophical realism justified by the critique can still be considered an immediate realism.

This question is far from easy to resolve. At first glance, any philosopher who claims descent from Aristotle will be surprised to hear that the existence of the external world cannot be validly proven except by means of evidence which is considered prior to philosophy and which passes judgment upon philosophy. This is not just a matter of fidelity to tradition. The tradition itself is founded upon philosophical necessities that can be grasped with a little effort. It is not hard to see that a realism based upon a critique that is distinct from realism itself, far from being immediate, will have only a conditional validity, dependent in the last analysis upon the critique that justifies it. In other words, we will be sure of apprehending immediately a reality independent of our thought, but we will not be immediately certain.

An immediate critical realism whose philosophical validity is not immediately evident may not be self-contradictory, but it is certainly a confused and equivocal notion, as we will try to show. On the one hand, this realism emphatically asserts that it does not presuppose the critique that justifies it. Quite to the contrary, the critique itself presupposes a knowledge of reality which cannot be dispensed with for a single second. Thus the critique is purely and exclusively reflexive and therefore secondary.[4] Consequently, we are here concerned with a critique of realism from within that very realism. On the other hand, if our apprehension of reality is primary, it will condition the reflection which renders it explicit and, as a result, this reflection will not constitute a point of view distinct from the realism it is supposed to judge. In short, because it has always presupposed realism, it will never have criticized realism. If immediate critical realism is to survive, it must constantly shift between two distinct positions which use the same name. "Immediate realism" will then signify the immediate apprehension of an external reality distinct from thought. If it is objected that such a realism is not critical,

---

[4] J. Maritain, *Les Degrés du savoir* (Paris: Desclée), 143–45. Cf. L. Noël, "Les Progrès de l'épistémologie thomiste", 442–43.

the answer will be that it is, because the validity of this apprehension is affirmed only in virtue of a critical reflection. And if it is objected that it is no longer immediate since it depends upon a critique, the answer will be that the object of the critique is precisely to manifest the immediate character of the realism.

There is a difficulty in all this, however. If we begin by admitting that our immediate apprehension of the existence of external beings is immediately self-evident, it will still be possible to carry out a philosophical reflection upon that immediate self-evidence, but at no point will our immediate apprehension have been criticized or judged. A judgment that expresses what is evident cannot itself be judged. In order for an immediate realism to be able to characterize itself as critical it will be necessary to justify its affirmation of the external world by means of a prior affirmation which is even more immediately valid. In short, as far as its certitude is concerned, the affirmation of the external world will depend upon the affirmation of an existence which is somehow better known.

Here we find the real problem presented, stripped of all nonessentials: is this realism of the external world sufficient without its critique? Once the question is framed in this way it must be answered with a yes or no. To say that the critique presupposes a philosophy but that, after the critique, "all our philosophical affirmations are transposed and acquire a new validity" is the same as saying that without the critique philosophy is not possessed of that degree of certainty that we might wish for it. Now, in discussing the existence of the external world any amount of wavering or uncertainty, no matter how small, not only affects all of philosophy but also changes the nature of the response given.

When we are told that the critique bestows a new certitude upon the affirmations of immediate realism we may take it as understood that, left to its own resources, realism is unable to stand on its own and is not self-evident. But then a whole series of unavoidable consequences will follow, the first of which is that if we do not take the immediately self-evident existence of external beings as our starting point, it will be necessary to start with the existence of thought alone. To proceed from thought to being in any sense whatsoever is to follow an idealist methodology. And so immediate realism is condemned to fall into either idealism or self-contradiction.

In point of fact, immediate realism spontaneously becomes self-contradictory. In order to justify its pretensions to the title "critical" it became necessary to find an "incontestable starting point" upon which realism could be based. This starting point had to be distinct from realism itself because the whole problem was to base realism upon something that would justify it. It is hardly surprising, then, that Descartes should have furnished such a starting point and that the *cogito* should have been called to the aid of immediate realism as the incontestable starting point which this doctrine needed.[5]

We will not pause over this paradoxical turn of events, since we will have many opportunities to return to it. What must be stressed at this point is that if, in such a doctrine, the *cogito* is chosen as the sole unquestionable starting point of philosophy, even of a realist philosophy, we may rest assured that all other starting points are very questionable indeed. *Cogito* — I think — and behold the incontestable starting point, for "nothing is more intimately linked to thought than thought itself. When it grasps itself in the act

[5] "It is a question of satisfying the requirement laid down by modern philosophy since Descartes, which seeks to base philosophy firmly upon an incontestable starting point. This starting point customarily goes under the name of the Cartesian *cogito*" (L. Noël, "La Méthode du réalisme", 437).

of reflection it attains a degree of certitude which is free from any possibility of doubt. From this starting point we will be able to conduct a methodical reconstruction of knowledge."[6] If the *cogito* is to enjoy this privilege of unquestionability, the *res sunt* must be excluded. If the *res sunt* does not enjoy this privilege, it can be doubted. If it can be doubted, immediate realism admits the possibility of doubting the existence of the external world. So it becomes necessary to resurrect not only the *cogito* but also the Cartesian doubt. If the *cogito* is the one incontestable starting point for philosophy, the rest may be doubted. The existence of extramental beings will no longer be indubitably self-evident unless it is submitted to the perfect self-evidence of the *cogito*. When such doctrines penetrate an epistemology which not only calls itself realist (although critical) but also Thomist, the problem of their introduction within the Aristotelian tradition becomes acutely evident. The only way to solve the problem is to attribute some type of methodic doubt, that is, some sort of *cogito*, to St. Thomas. We will now examine two attempts to solve the problem in this way.

I. THOMISM'S METHODIC DOUBT

The idea that some form of methodic doubt can be found in the writings of Aristotle and St. Thomas was first advanced several years ago and has gained considerable support among philosophers since then. Today, this idea is accepted by the majority of neo-scholastic philosophers in search of a critique, and I can hardly give a better picture of the present state of affairs than by quoting the following passage:

[6] Ibid.

Aristotle had already made methodic doubt the necessary preface to true science, and at the outset of his metaphysics he required a thoroughgoing doubt . . . a doubt which would gather together all difficulties. . . . Thomas Aquinas, in his commentary upon this passage, took up the same theme and stressed it with remarkable vigor. The following passage certainly makes it clear that the first condition for a metaphysics is a universal, methodic doubt: "Aliae scientiae considerant particulariter de veritate, unde et particulariter ad eas pertinet circa singulas veritates dubitare. Sed ista scientia sicut habet universalem considerationem de veritate, ita etiam ad eam pertinet universalis dubitatio de veritate."[7]

For a long time many philosophers felt that the best way to handle this argument was to say nothing about it. Unfortunately, it received such a favorable reception that it has become impossible to remain silent without being accused either of ignoring the argument or of fearing its strength. Therefore, let us first determine the meaning of the text from Aristotle to which we are referred and then compare the text with the proposed interpretation of it.

At the beginning of book B of the *Metaphysics*, Aristotle observes that "it is necessary, in the interests of the science we are seeking, to begin by first considering the problems we will have to discuss."[8] These problems are those concerning

[7] To our knowledge, this argument was first raised by L. Noël in 1913: "Le Problème de la connaissance", reproduced in *Notes d'épistémologie thomiste*, 19–50. It was used again by the same author in *Réalisme méthodique ou réalisme critique*, 116. We reproduced this last text.

[8] Aristotle, *Métaphysique* B, 1, 995a 24–25. We cite the translation by J. Tricot (Aristotle, *Métaphysique*, [Paris: J. Vrin, 1933], 1:69), not only because it is a happy combination of fidelity to the original and readability, but also because no one will be able to suspect that it was done with the intention of justifying our interpretation of the text in question.

which "certain philosophers have expounded a doctrine different from our own and, in addition, those problems which seem to have been neglected." In other words, Aristotle felt that before going on to an exposition of his own doctrine he should enumerate and define those problems which his doctrine would have to resolve. These problems were of two kinds: those which had been positions held by earlier philosophers and which Aristotle intended to contradict, and those which had not been considered by his predecessors and which he himself intended to consider. Several factors make such a procedure advisable. First, it is impossible to resolve a difficulty without having defined the nature of the difficulty to be resolved, just as "it is impossible to untie a knot without knowing how it was tied." Now "to be perplexed is, for thought, much the same as the condition of a man in chains: it can no more continue on its way than he can."[9] In short, the first reason for beginning by defining and discussing these problems is that, until they have been resolved, thought is bound by them and is unable to proceed directly to an exposition of the truth.

Aristotle adds a second reason to the first, namely, that "to search for an answer without first posing the problem is like setting out without knowing where you are going; you will never know whether or not you have found what you were looking for. Obviously, in such a case you will be proceeding without any objective, and the only way to gain a clear idea of what the objective is, is to first discuss the difficulties that must be resolved." The third and last reason for proceeding in this *sic et non* manner is that "you will necessarily be in a better position to judge the question when you have understood all the opposing arguments, much as in a judicial proceeding."[10]

[9] Aristotle, op. cit., 1:70.
[10] Ibid.

From this text we can see that for Aristotle the study and orderly exposition of metaphysics presupposes an examination of certain problems. These problems are essentially four in number, although there are numerous ancillary problems (Aristotle lists fourteen immediately after the text cited above).[11] Of the four, only one, the second, bears directly upon what is today called noetics or the theory of knowledge. It poses the question of whether metaphysics should "consider only the first principles of substance or also . . . deal with the general principles of demonstration, such as: is it possible to affirm and deny the same thing at the same time, and other similar principles."[12] The other thirteen problems have to do with causality, the Ideas, genera and species, the number and nature of the principles of things, etc.; in other words, these problems presuppose a theory of knowledge, although they are not themselves directly concerned with it. We might also add that the second problem is not presented as a problem concerning knowledge but as one of the problems which are related to the object of metaphysics or, more exactly, which are an extension of that object. So, up to this point we have found nothing remotely resembling the Cartesian doubt in this text. The only question presented is one of method, in the ordinary sense of the order to be followed in a discussion.

It can be clearly seen from the preceding that, far from being presented as a preliminary critique which must be conducted before beginning metaphysics, the difficulties concerning the principles of demonstration are only cited in the second place. After asking whether one science or several should study the different kinds of causes, Aristotle simply adds: "But are the principles of demonstration, with the

[11] For a list of these questions, consult Aristotle, op. cit., 70–73; also W. D. Ross, *Aristotle's Metaphysics* (Oxford, 1934), 1:221–22.

[12] Aristotle, *Métaphysique*, trans. J. Tricot, 70–71.

causes, the object of a single science or of several? That also is a problem."[13] And, we might add, it is a problem of the same type as the preceding one, since Aristotle's only concern here is to decide which problems metaphysics should deal with before going forward with an exposition of metaphysics proper.

If anyone has any doubts concerning what I have said, they need only reread the chapter. Basically, Aristotle says that the first principles are known by an immediate experience, and every science uses them and treats them as established truths. Therefore, they are not the property of any particular science, and no science assumes the task of discussing these truths. On the other hand, if the philosopher does not deal with these principles, who will? And if it is not possible to discuss them in any of the particular sciences treating of the nature of things, what science will be assigned this task? Here we have the pro and con; in fact Aristotle poses the problem twice in book B before resolving it in book G of the *Metaphysics*.[14] We will later consider his solution in order to determine its meaning. For the present we need only state the nature of the question, and its nature has nothing whatsoever to do with the doubt, be it methodic or otherwise, which some philosophers think must be cast upon all knowledge before we may be certain of the first principle. On the contrary, Aristotle declares that all the sciences before metaphysics have validly used these principles, considering them to be self-evident. The only real question here is, when we take up the study of the principles themselves, which science will be qualified to do

[13] Aristotle, *Métaphysique*, B, 2, 996b 26–27; trans. J. Tricot, 1:76.
[14] The problem is first formulated in summary fashion in *Métaphysique*, B, 1, 995b 10–13; then it is discussed under various aspects at B, 2, 996b 26–997 a15; it is finally resolved at G, 3, 1004b 18–1005b 34.

so? This is all Aristotle had to say on the matter, and whoever adds to it must take full responsibility. Does St. Thomas add anything further in his commentary? Some of his interpreters would have it so.[15] It is true that, whatever it may mean, St. Thomas' text does seem at first to have a vague Cartesian quality about it which is not present in Aristotle's text. This may be attributed to the fact that the Greek terms ἀπορία and ἀπορῆσαι are translated into Latin by *dubitatio* and *dubitare*. When St. Thomas begins speaking about a *universalis dubitatio de veritate* the formula suggests so vividly a universal doubt concerning the possibility of truth in general that it is difficult not to read into it an invitation to some kind of critical enterprise analogous to the Cartesian methodic doubt. First impressions can be deceptive, however. We must examine the meaning of these expressions more carefully.

In the strict sense, ἀπορία, an *uporia*, is "a confrontation between two contrary and equally well-reasoned opinions in response to the same question."[16] The Latin word *dubitatio* has retained this sense, at least as one of its possible meanings. In the Middle Ages a *dubitatio* could be a doubt, but it could also be a problem, a difficulty or a question. A *bona dubitatio* is a good question, an interesting question worth examining. Before attributing to St. Thomas the concept of a universal doubt comparable to Descartes', it would be well to determine first what meaning he himself attributed to the word *dubitatio* in this passage.

To tell the truth, the passage would not have presented

---

[15] "And Thomas Aquinas' commentary upon this passage (from Aristotle) accentuates it with remarkable vigor" (L. Noël, *Réalisme méthodique ou réalisme critique*, 116).

[16] O. Hamelin, *Le Système d'Aristote* (Paris: F. Alcan, 223); cited by J. Tricot, trans. cit., 1:69.

any problem if it had not been approached with the intention of reconciling it with Descartes. St. Thomas wrote the passage in question as part of his commentary on the *Metaphysics* of Aristotle. His principal concern when he wrote the commentary was to explain Aristotle's text, not to surreptitiously insert a doctrine so strange in spirit and novel in content as a doubt of the Cartesian type would have been. In fact, he seems to have limited his effort in this case to precisely those bounds, and this can be seen as long as the passage is not used to support a doctrine it was never intended to support. Aristotle, we are told, required, at the very outset of metaphysics, "a thoroughgoing doubt: τὸ διαπορῆσαι καλῶς. . .",[17] but τὸ διαπορῆσαι καλῶς does not mean "a thoroughgoing doubt"; it simply means, as Tricot's very accurate translation puts it, "to develop an ἀπορία with care" or, in other words, to define exactly the problem which is to be resolved.

Or at least that is how St. Thomas interpreted it, and that, for the moment, is all that concerns us. For him *bene dubitare* means simply "bene attingere ad ea quae sunt dubitabilia. Et hoc ideo quia posterior investigatio veritatis, nihil aliud est quam solutio prius dubitatorum." If you do not know how the knot was tied, you will not be able to untie it. If you are to succeed, you must first examine the rope and determine what type of knot has been used. Only then will you be able to untie the knot and move on. It is the same with reason when it is confronted with an ἀπορία (*dubitatio*). Every ἀπορία, every unsolved problem, has the same effect upon the reason as physical bonds have on the body. A man who *dubitat*, that is, who does not know how to resolve a problem, is like a man whose feet are bound:

---

[17] L. Noël, *Réalisme méthodique ou réalisme critique*, 116.

"Ille qui dubitat, quasi habens mentem ligatam, non potest ad anteriora procedere secundum viam speculationis." What is needed in order to move forward once again? It is necessary to *solvere dubitationem*, to leave uncertainty behind and liberate the mind from the unresolved problems which encumber it. To do that, *oportet quod prius speculetur omnes difficultates et earum causas*.[18] In short, in order to move forward with the study of metaphysics, it is first necessary to examine all ἀπορίαι, all the problems which, properly speaking, precede the actual exposition of the subject. Up to this point, St. Thomas' commentary is in perfect agreement with Aristotle's text.

The rest of the commentary does not raise any special problem. St. Thomas simply points out and underlines the processes of Aristotle's reasoning. Whoever wishes to search for the truth *non considerando prius dubitationem* (which emphatically does *not* mean "without doubting" but rather "without first ascertaining the difficulty which is preventing progress") is like someone who starts out on a trip without having a destination. For the traveller the end of the trip comes when he reaches the place for which he set out. For one in search of truth the end is the *exclusio dubitationis*. But to eliminate a problem it is first necessary to see it, for even if the traveller arrives at his destination by chance, he will not realize that he *has* arrived: "Ita etiam quando aliquis non praecognoscit dubitationem, cujus solutio est finis inquisitionis, non potest scire quando invenit veritatem quaesitam, et quando non." Clearly, we are not dealing with a doubt but with a difficulty or problem. St. Thomas' point is that we must at least be aware of the problem in order to recognize a solution to it.

[18] Thomas Aquinas, *In Metaphysicam Aristotelis*, bk. 3, lect. 1; Cathala ed., n. 339.

Finally, while clarifying what he calls Aristotle's fourth reason, St. Thomas observes that it is the master's job to resolve the problems raised by disputants. No judge can render a verdict without first having understood the positions of both parties. Likewise, the student of philosophy will also be better able to make a judgment when he has understood all the reasoning involved, especially when two adversaries have presented their respective points of view in the form of a debate: "Si audierit omnes rationes quasi adversariorum dubitantium."[19] This text presupposes that the actual disputation took place in front of the students, bringing the ἀπορία or *dubitatio* to life before their eyes.

Should anyone still entertain the least doubt on this subject he need only read the following passage from the commentary in order to dispel it. "We must note", St. Thomas adds,

> that this is the reason why, in almost all his books, Aristotle generally reviewed the issues which were raised before determining the truth of the matter. But in his other books he introduces each question one by one rather than presenting all the issues together, as he does here. The reason is that, while other sciences consider particular aspects of the truth and so naturally consider each particular problem as it arises, this science, since it considers truth in its universality (*sicut habet universalem considerationem de veritate*), must present the problem of truth in its universality (*ita etiam ad eam pertinet universalis dubitatio de veritate*). This is why, instead of examining each problem separately, he examines them all at the same time (*et ideo non particulariter, sed simul universalem dubitationem prosequitur*).[20]

[19] Thomas Aquinas, op. cit., n. 340–42.

[20] Thomas Aquinas, op. cit., n. 343. If anyone has any lingering doubts about the correct Thomist meaning of this word, just read the following text: "Postulat a me vestra dilectio, ut de articulis fidei et

St. Thomas is, of course, giving his own opinion and in the process adding another reason to the four already advanced by Aristotle, but he only does so in order to explain the fact that Aristotle bunched all the problems dealt with in metaphysics into book B of the *Metaphysics* instead of presenting them as he dealt with them throughout the course of the whole work. The explanation which St. Thomas suggests is that metaphysics, since it deals with the problem of truth in general rather than with this or that truth, must enumerate in one place every ἀπορία relating to the object of metaphysics. Now, some might say that this is a rather elaborate explanation for a simple fact, and perhaps it is, but it is precisely what St. Thomas wishes to say. His intention is so clearly to explain why book B presents all the problems and the following books provide the solutions that he goes right on to propose another explanation which leads us to the heart of the *Metaphysics*: almost all the *dubitabilia* or contested positions which he enumerates are positions which were held by other philosophers and which he opposes. Now, these philosophers proceeded from the intelligible to the sensible, while Aristotle in his pursuit of truth invariably proceeded from the sensible to the intelligible. Thus, the order which Aristotle followed in his search for truth was the reverse of the order other philosophers had

---

Ecclesiae sacramentis aliqua vobis compendio se pro memoriali transcriberem, cum *dubitationibus* quae circa haec moveri possent" (De articulis fidei, init., in *Opuscula Omnia*, ed. P. Mandonnet, 3:1). St. Thomas adds that every theological undertaking bears "*circa dubitates contingentes articulos fidei*". From which it follows that if *dubitatio* equals doubt, every theological study will deal with doubts which may be raised concerning the articles of faith. The obvious meaning of the text is: you ask me to write you something concerning the articles of faith and the sacraments, with the problems that may arise in considering this subject.

followed. This accounts for his decision to list all the difficulties involved in their doctrines in one place, for since he could not simultaneously expound his own positions and criticize theirs, he preferred to list all their positions separately at the beginning of his book and then discuss them according to the order of his own doctrine: ideo praelegit primo ponere dubitationes omnes seorsum, et postea suo ordine dubitationes determinare.[21]

We are now able to list the points of agreement between St. Thomas and Descartes. We have been assured that their agreement is not *merely* verbal.[22] Actually, it is not *even* verbal, for nobody has shown us a single instance in which Descartes spoke of a *universalis dubitatio de veritate* as St. Thomas did, nor any instance in which St. Thomas said, as Descartes did: "I thought that it was necessary . . . to reject as absolutely false anything concerning which I was able to entertain the least doubt."[23] The only point of contact that we have been shown is that they both use the words *dubitatio* and *dubitare,* but in different senses. It will not do to say that "in the following chapters of the *Metaphysics* Aristotle does not develop the methodic doubt in the same way as Descartes did."[24] The truth is that Aristotle's ἀπορία and St. Thomas' *dubitatio* have nothing whatsoever to do with the Cartesian doubt. Aristotle's and St. Thomas'

[21] Thomas Aquinas, op. cit., n. 344. Note 345 adds a third reason for the same facts, which St. Thomas borrows from Averroes: "Tertiam assignat Averroes dicens hoc esse propter affinitatem hujus scientiae ad logicam, quae tangitur infra in quarto. Et ideo dialecticam disputationem posuit circa partes principales hujus scientiae."

[22] L. Noël, *Réalisme méthodique ou réalisme critique,* 117.

[23] R. Descartes, *Discours de la méthode,* part 4, ed. Adam-Tannery, 6: 31, l. 26–30.We might note in passing that the expression "methodic doubt" is not found in Descartes' text.

[24] L. Noël, *Réalisme méthodique ou réalisme critique,* 117.

"doubt" actually refers only to the questions presented, but Descartes' doubt runs to the answers given to the questions. At the beginning of their metaphysics Aristotle and St. Thomas present a number of questions one after the other so as not to forget to answer them. At the beginning of his metaphysics Descartes decrees that every response given by other sciences to their proper questions must be considered false because the new metaphysics has not justified them yet. There is no similarity between the two positions.

This is undoubtedly the reason why those who would try to reconcile the two positions seem so undiscriminating when it comes to finding points of comparison. Still, if they were determined to talk about resemblances between the two philosophies they should have come forward with at least one genuine example. To say that the two resemble each other in that they both present all the problems so as to uncover any confusion "in order to progress in the full light to that which is not mixed with shade" is to say nothing that could not be said equally well, if not of every philosopher, at least of every metaphysician. Every metaphysician knows how to present questions in the most general manner possible "until there are no more questions to ask". What is important is to show that the manner in which they pose these ultimate questions is somehow similar. Now, Descartes' doubt is the very opposite of the method followed by Aristotle and St. Thomas. It will not do to say that, whereas Aristotle "tries to gather all the difficulties together in order to be fully aware of those points which need to have light shed upon them, Descartes tries to attain the luminous summit from which he will be able to carry out, with absolute clarity, the first forward step of the mind and from which he will then be able to reconstruct, with the same absolute clarity, the whole edifice of knowledge."[25] Such vague formulas only serve to avoid the real question by attempting to baptize the most profound differences. For it is precisely because Descartes tries to attain that luminous summit that he must doubt all the rest. And it is precisely because St. Thomas does not try to do so that he never needs to doubt everything else.

These two methods disagree in so many respects that they are totally incompatible, as was the case with Aristotle and his predecessors. For Aristotle and St. Thomas, the first principle is at work even in the most humble of true judgments, and when metaphysics has progressed to the point that it is a fitting crown for all the other sciences it does not set itself up as the sole starting point from which the rest of the sciences must be deduced if they are to have any validity. A Thomist would never doubt the validity of mathematics simply because he had not yet constructed a metaphysics. For him, every rational being is naturally in possession of the first principle and makes valid use of it in all branches of learning, even though he may be ignorant of the correct metaphysical formula or even of the very existence of the first principle. As a matter of fact, the world is full of people who are engaged in science but are not aspiring to wisdom. They never give a thought to the first principles, yet they use them and their science suffers not at all for the lack of conscious attention to the first principles of knowledge. In Descartes' philosophy, however, nobody may use the first principle without having consciously considered it. This is so true, in fact, that until this is done every science, even mathematics, must be considered doubtful. The methodic doubt is therefore the necessary antecedent condition for the discovery of the first principle, for the first principle can be

[25] Ibid.

recognized by the fact that it, and it alone, is able to resist successfully the test posed by methodic doubt. In short, we must doubt everything in order to discover the one thing that cannot be doubted, and because it cannot be doubted it will be the first principle of knowledge.

In a controversy of this sort it is of the utmost importance to know if the same name is being used to designate two different philosophical positions. For Aristotelian and Thomistic philosophy, the first principle is coessential with the first act of the human intellect. It is validly used to advance the sciences until it comes into the clear light of self-consciousness in metaphysics, the peak of human knowledge. On the other hand, for Cartesian philosophy the discovery of the first principle is the necessary condition of all valid knowledge. Thus, metaphysics is the *source* of all the sciences rather than their crowning perfection. In the first case it is, of course, necessary to examine all the problems proper to metaphysics, and it may be expedient to formulate them all at one time, but in no sense, at no moment does metaphysics presuppose a universal doubt or a special power which enables the intellect to attain truth and being. In the second case, however, it is first necessary to doubt everything in order to discover the first principle. These two positions are worlds apart, and they cannot be reconciled without distorting the essence of one or the other or both.

One might well ask if this is not exactly what happened. It is truly surprising to observe the imprudence with which certain realists handle the essential theses of Cartesianism without seeming to realize that they are playing with explosives that must inevitably destroy their realism. Far from seeing that the methodic doubt is inseparable from Cartesian idealism, they think that the effort of modern philosophy to attain a first principle by means of methodic doubt offers the advantage of giving philosophy a systematic and linear structure "in which everything follows logically, on the model of geometry. This is the ideal found in the rules Descartes adopted in his quest. Ideal, perhaps too rigid, but it was right for him to try to come as close as possible to that ideal."[26] The result can be foreseen, in error and truth alike, as soon as the abstract necessity of essences comes into play. Whoever accepts a Cartesian first principle must also accept the methodic doubt. Only in this way can philosophy attain that linear structure which the first principle promises to bestow upon it. For a philosophy is linear insofar as it is deductive, and it is deductive to the extent that it is idealist. Since St. Thomas' philosophy is strictly realist it does not have a linear or mathematical structure, nor can it be deduced from a single principle, attained at the price of methodic doubt. It is possible merely to borrow Descartes' formulas without paying attention to what they mean, but that is more an opportunism than a philosophy and ceases to interest us. But if, even without being bound to maintain their original meaning intact, you seek to preserve a part of it, you can be sure that sooner or later these formulas will lead back to the essentials of Cartesianism: the very negation of Aristotle's and St. Thomas' realism.

II. THE THOMIST COGITO

After receiving an able send-off from Monsignor Noël, the Thomistic methodic doubt has continued to gain ground. It was immediately adopted by G. Picard, then by M.-D. Roland-Gosselin and by J. Maréchal, so that, P. Descoqs tells

---

[26] Ibid.

us, it now receives general acceptance: "Idem nunc magis atque magis apud scholasticos admittitur."[27] It is not surprising, then, that after witnessing the rapid growth of a scholastic methodic doubt we should now be confronted with a scholastic or Thomist *cogito*. It is certainly not by chance that Descartes started with doubt and continued *with the cogito*. Nor is it by chance that, having started with the one, Descartes' scholastic imitators should proceed to the other. The necessary relationship between the two theses is as binding for them as it was for him, and no philosopher who is concerned with logical consistency can long avoid this necessity.

It is certainly a serious matter to accept the first principle of a metaphysics while intending to reject the consequences of that principle. The risk is all the more serious in this case for we are dealing with philosophies which claim that their elements are linked with an absolute necessity in a quasi-geometrical fashion. This explains the hesitancy of those who attempt to proceed in this manner. As soon as they see undesirable consequences flowing from the Cartesian first principle, the very consequences which Descartes had embraced, they promptly claim that they are putting the principle to a totally different use and that, really, they understand it in a totally different sense. But if one objects that it is now no longer the same principle and that the discussion has become a word game, they restore to the principle some

---

[27] L. Noël, "Le Réalisme immédiat", in *Revue néoscolastique* (May 1923), 163 (reproduced in *Notes d'épistémologie thomiste* [Louvain and Paris: G. Beauchesne, 1923], 77). M. D. Roland-Gosselin, in *Bulletin thomiste,* (May 1925), 80. J. Maréchal, *Le Point de départ de la métaphysique,* Notebook 5 (Louvain and Paris, 1925), 38–40. P. Descoqs, *Praelectiones théologiae naturalis* (Paris: G. Beauchesne, 1932), 1:45–57. The list is not complete.

of its proper sense at the risk of being saddled with the consequences they were trying to avoid. Nothing can prevent someone from shifting between these two positions indefinitely. In order to circumscribe a ground upon which a conversation may be conducted using a constant sense for the words, let us state that we see no practical difficulty in introducing into Thomism a methodic doubt which is neither a doubt nor methodic. Nor do we see any practical impossibility in adopting the Cartesian *cogito* as a first principle, as long as it is not used as a principle and retains none of its original Cartesian meaning. In certain neo-scholastic works this seems to be all that is involved. The authors simply amuse themselves by adopting the outward trappings of modern philosophy. Such a posture does not even come close to the point where a philosophical discussion may begin. But there are other neo-scholastic philosophies in which the essential and primary character of their principle is respected and accepted for what it is, although an attempt is made to restrict the scope of the principle involved. The following discussion is directed only toward this latter type of philosophy and only insofar as this attitude is adopted.

It is precisely because he takes these ideas so seriously that Monsignor L. Noël, having conceded the necessity of a methodic doubt, finds himself naturally led, as was Descartes, to make this a doubt that runs to any answer given and not merely a doubt that is really just a question. Of course, that is to be expected, for the *vis verborum* requires it. To doubt does not mean simply to question. Once you start to doubt you inevitably end up doing just what the word means: considering all possible answers to the question as at least provisionally uncertain. Thus, having accepted Descartes' methodic doubt, Monsignor Noël finds himself accepting the same philosopher's precise reason for doubting:

"This is therefore the goal of the Cartesian effort, the result of the methodic doubt. It is necessary that the new philosophy have a carefully defined starting point of which it is fully possessed, its stronghold, and this will be the first principle of philosophy."[28] Now, if you are looking for a first principle in the Cartesian sense, that is, a first judgment of existence which no doubt can disturb, you will find yourself naturally led to the same principle Descartes used: thought. All may be attained by means of it, and without it we can achieve nothing: "For a systematic philosophy, thought is not simply one among many possible starting points. It is, we think, the only legitimate starting point."[29]

We have come a long way since we started. Since setting out to find a critical realism we have also discovered, by means of the methodic doubt, a systematic philosophy constructed on a linear pattern by starting from that which is easiest to know and, as a consequence, founded upon some sort of *cogito*. If that is Thomistic epistemology then nothing is impossible, and no one need any longer fear to present the following thesis in the name of Thomism: "All epistemology as well as the starting point of metaphysics is contained herein, and the fate of metaphysics hangs upon the answer to the question: is it or is it not possible to reach actually existing beings while starting with the *cogito*?"[30] It

[28] L. Noël, *Réalisme méthodique ou réalisme critique*, 118.

[29] L. Noël, op. cit., 119–20.

[30] L. Noël, *Notes d'épistémologie thomiste*, 188. Some might fear that this text, isolated from its proper context, does not really mean what it says. The truth is that we have made it say less than it actually does: "We have already explained (55) how the Cartesian doubt, touching upon the most universal questions, has led the mind to the initial point of view expressed in the *cogito*, made more precise by three centuries of criticism: the mind turning back upon itself, grasping itself by reflection without any intermediary and seeking to define the value and meaning of its own

is necessary to be absolutely certain as to just what we are talking about. If you really think that thought is the only legitimate starting point for metaphysics, that this starting point contains the whole of epistemology and that it is possible to reach existing beings from such a starting point, then you have the right to say so. But, since St. Thomas never used thought as a starting point, never founded his epistemology upon thought and never had to use it in order to reach existence, what reason can anyone advance for calling this collection of basic positions Thomist? In reality, they are totally Cartesian and have nothing whatsoever to do with St. Thomas. The only state of mind that could account for this hodgepodge and give it at least a semblance of intelligibility would be an intent to compromise.

The first step in a realist *cogito* is the observation that the object grasped by thought is distinct from thought itself. As Lachelier wrote, "Everything that is an object of thought is other than the act of thought itself." Still, this object of thought will not get us beyond thought unless it is derived directly from the real object: "Realism can only be justified in this way. Immediate realism does indeed affirm that this is so, but can it really prove this?"[31] There are those who insist that such a proof is possible. After all, they say, we do have a concept of "the real", and it must come from somewhere. It comes to us from what is given to us in thought as independent of or, better, not dependent upon our thought. For this is what we mean by "the real": "While ideas are experienced as dependent upon conscious activity, reality is

---

acts. This is the whole of epistemology. . ." etc. Thus, after three centuries of criticism, the *cogito* will become the obligatory starting point for the new Thomist epistemology.

[31] L. Noël, *Réalisme méthodique ou réalisme critique*, 124.

not experienced as dependent upon conscious activity."[32] All of these formulas are manifestly equivocal and, from Plato to Malebranche, through Plotinus and St. Augustine, they have served generations of thinkers as reasons for depreciating the reality of the external world in order to exalt the reality of the Ideas. We may simply note that this is not Fr. Noël's meaning; for him, the reality which is given to us "is the sensibly given which consciousness finds continually confronting it and asserting itself as coming from outside, . . . to which we may or may not pay attention but which can neither be created nor suppressed".[33]

Here we have finally come full circle, but the reader will be excused if he wonders why so much effort was expended creating the sensation of movement when in reality we have gone nowhere. First, we were told that we had to carry out an exhaustive, methodic doubt, but, since we were not permitted to doubt either thought or the fact of the existence of sensible reality, what did we actually doubt? Descartes' doubt at least doubts something, but Monsignor Noël's doubts nothing. Then the *cogito* was posited as the only possible starting point for metaphysics, although Monsignor Noël was careful to add that extramental reality is always present in thought. If extramental reality is immediately given, the *cogito* can hardly be prior to it and, since the two are equally present, each contained within the other, in what sense can the *cogito* be posited as the only possible starting point? Then we were told that the fate of metaphysics would be decided by the answer to this question: "Is it or is it not possible to reach existing beings by means of the *cogito*?" But if reality is immediately present to thought, it is contradictory to start with thought in order to gain

[32] L. Noël, op. cit., 127–28.
[33] L. Noël, op. cit., 128.

reality. You cannot cross a bridge that does not exist. All this amounts to is a sham battle between an ineffectual method and nonexistent difficulties, for it must be stated clearly that the "open *cogito*" which is supposed to be opposed to Descartes' "closed *cogito*"[34] is nothing but an optical illusion. When Descartes says that he starts from the "I think", what he says has a definite meaning because he does, in fact, start with thought alone. This is why neither he nor his successors were able to escape from the pit into which they had dug themselves. But to say that you will start from the "I think" while including the existence of the external world in the formula is simply to start from the very place for which you pretended to set out.

Who would have expected a realist to attempt to deceive his opponents with this intellectual sleight of hand? It so happens, however, that he deceived himself. Here, as always, the problems start with a poorly calculated reaction against "common-sense" realisms. These realisms, which are believed to be philosophically grounded without even being reflective, are set up in opposition to reflection, as if every reflective act is Cartesian and therefore critical. Now, every critique is reflective, but every reflective act is not necessarily critical. Because he assumes the contrary, Monsignor Noël considers a realism founded upon the *cogito* to be critical and thinks that his own *cogito* qualifies as a critical method. A very simple critique, however, for it consists of becoming aware that what is immediately evident for thought is, indeed, immediately evident. Since his *cogito* states that it is not necessary to pass from thought to being it will end up saying that there is nothing to criticize.

[34] L. Noël, "L'Epistémologie thomiste", in *Acta secundi congr. thomist. internat.*, 34. On this subject, see the just remarks by J. Maritain, op. cit., 42–43.

In the final analysis that is exactly what happens to this subtle dialectic, and philosophy has little to show for the effort expended. Since immediate realism is the only realism worthy of the name, those who are in agreement on this point also agree as to the structure of reality. The more assured they feel of being correct, the more they strive to avoid harming such an important truth. Philosophy was treated very shabbily indeed when it was recommended that philosophers accept realism as simply a truth of common sense, for the truths of common sense are not all philosophically self-evident. However, it was certainly no better to disguise realism as its very opposite in the hope of making it more acceptable to modern tastes. In the first place such an undertaking is not worthy of realism nor even, for that matter, of the error being combatted. When viewed in their original context the expressions which Monsignor Noël borrowed from Descartes designate carefully delineated operations of thought which are all directed against immediate realism, such as Monsignor Noël has quite correctly conceived of it. If you refuse to perform these operations, what sense is there in using the expressions which Descartes created to designate them? When Descartes insists that we use the methodic doubt he is opposing the evidence of sensation, even that which testifies to the existence of the external world; what sort of methodic doubt is forbidden to doubt this? Descartes starts with the *cogito*, above all, in order to show that the external world is not immediately given in that thought; how, then, can the *cogito* be the necessary condition of all metaphysical knowledge if the *res sunt* is also immediately known? Rather than openly maintaining that the existence of the external world is evident only if the existence of thought is first grasped, Monsignor Noël's whole idealist dialectic requires, as the indispensable condition of a truly philosophical realism, that we borrow the names of these Cartesian operations without having the slightest intention of carrying them out.

This is why, with all due respect to its defenders, I continue to think that "the problem of establishing a realist critique is self-contradictory, just like the notion of a square circle."[35] An old scholastic saw, so well known as to seem hackneyed, perhaps, has it that *ab esse ad nosse valet consequentia*. I hope I will be excused for recalling it, but these words express the essence of any true realism. You can start with thought or with being, but you cannot do both at the same time. If you wish to construct a Thomistic epistemology, everyone knows that you must start with being. The first philosopher who dared to reverse this proposition was Descartes, for whom, according to his own expression, *a nosse ad esse valet consequentia*. He even adds that this is the only type of result that is valid. If you wish to avoid ambiguity it is here that a stand must be taken. To call a realism which proceeds from being to thought "critical" empties the word of all meaning. Such a realism cannot even be said to be contradictory, for although the definition contains two words, they refer to only one concept. But to say that "critical realism" is realist because in it reality is given immediately to thought yet that it is also critical because, as Monsignor Noël would have it, thought is for it "the only legitimate starting point", is to become involved in proving that *ab esse ad nosse valet consequentia* can be brought to the aid of the opposite proposition: *a nosse ad esse valet consequentia*. In short, as soon as the expression "critical realism" pretends to have any other meaning than "philosophical

---

[35] E. Gilson, *Le Réalisme méthodique*, 10. Contra: L. Noël, *Le Réalisme immédiat* (1938), 21–48.

realism", it becomes self-contradictory. The only case in which it is not self-contradictory is where it means nothing. What, then, is hidden behind immediate critical realism? Legitimate philosophical interests are, to be sure, but they can be much better expressed. Some seek to speak the language of their time in order to assure realism of an audience, but idealists who recognize this as a realism speaking in idealist language will simply conclude that its supporters do not know what they are talking about. Others seek to avoid presenting realism to critical idealists under the indefensible form of a naive realism, but if realism is to defend itself, it must first exist as a realism. The best means of assuring realism's survival is not to encumber a living doctrine with the cast-off and outmoded clothing of a doctrine that has been dead for three centuries.[36] That would truly be the best way to enter a discussion with adversaries who are only interested in Descartes insofar as he can be used against Aristotelian realism. Certainly it is far better than seeking to reconcile the two by decking realism in timeworn idealist clothing in which modern philosophers themselves no longer believe and which they refuse to call critical. The best way to defend classical realism is to become reacquainted with it in its totality and then make its whole intelligibility known to others.

[36] I cannot recommend enough the acute study from Karl Jasper's remarkable work "La Pensée de Descartes et la philosophie", in *Revue philosophique* (May-August, 1937), 39–148. We have presented our own point of view in E. Gilson, *The Unity of Philosophical Experience* (New York: Scribner's, 1937).

CHAPTER THREE

THE REALISM OF THE "I AM"

If you renounce the attempt to reach reality by means of a deductive process yet still insist that realism be critical, then the only conceivable access to reality for a position with this double requirement is by way of the *cogito*. The nature of the being apprehended by thought is of little consequence. As long as the apprehension is self-evident, the ability of thought to grasp reality, as it really is, is immediately guaranteed. Now, the critical problem is solved with the discovery of a guaranteed starting point. Therefore, if this guarantee can be found only in the *cogito*, we must necessarily have recourse to the immediate apprehension of thought by itself.

Fr. G. Picard seems to have considered this procedure to be the only safe course between the opposing claims of the various forms of skepticism and what he called absolute dogmatism. By "skepticism" Fr. Picard understands any doctrine which considers it impossible to attribute an absolute necessity to any knowledge whatsoever. By his definition, then, skepticism includes not only those positions which maintain that we can know nothing, that is, absolute skepticism but also what might be called phenomenalism: those schools of thought that maintain that all is appearance, all is relative, that nothing can be absolutely true. Also included in this definition is pragmatism, which maintains that the principles of knowledge are true if they are convenient. Thus, according to pragmatism we have motives rather than reasons for accepting the principles of knowledge.

Against any and every form of skepticism, absolute dogmatism opposes its unyielding affirmations.

> The mind, they say, by the very fact that it thinks, necessarily affirms its own reality beyond any possibility of a doubt, as well as affirming the reality of its object and its general competence in regard to its object. To think is, in effect, to posit being and to posit the mind as the proper faculty for apprehending being. By the simple fact that thought is thought, the mind affirms being and affirms its own status as the proper faculty for apprehending being, which amounts to the necessary affirmation of the objective value of reason.[1]

Therefore, the validity of knowledge simply is not a problem for dogmatisms of this type. The only problem is to decide which of our affirmations square with reality itself. This is not a critique of knowledge; it is simply a criteriology. Whether he wants to or not, the idealist must recognize the validity of reason as an instrument of knowledge. For him as for the realist it is only a question of discovering "which *criterium* is able to assure its correct application in different cases".[2]

Fr. Picard has directed his most biting criticisms against ultraintellectualist dogmatism's decision to reject the fundamental critical problem as illusory. Such a position, he tells us, confuses a factual question with the theoretical question which, properly speaking, is the beginning of philosophy. Every idealist will readily concede that, practically speaking, a spontaneous trust is implied in the normal

---

[1] G. Picard, "Le Problème critique fondamental", *Archives de Philosophie*, vol. I, report 2 (Paris: G. Beauchesne, 1923), 7.

[2] Ibid., 8.

operations of the mind, but the realist assumes that this trust is well founded while the idealist does not.

The ultimate reason advanced by the dogmatist is the subjective necessity of trusting the everyday operations of the mind, whereas we seek an objective standard that will justify the subjective necessity. If nothing better can be found we must work with what we have, and even then dogmatism will have the advantage over idealism because of its common-sense appeal. However, that will be its only advantage, and it will be inadequately armed to defend itself against either idealism or another form of dogmatism, whether excessively or insufficiently realistic.[3]

It is important to understand the problem as it was posed by Fr. Picard, for his initial posture controls the rest of the discussion. Clearly, his principal preoccupation is to make sure that common sense will not be the sole guarantor of realism. The simplest way to express this desire is to say that realism must be philosophical, for even if the bald assertions of common sense merit the attention of philosophy, they cannot be considered to have philosophical value. This is what Fr. Picard suggests when he tells us: "These observations show the importance of having a philosophical solution, even though imperfect, to the critical problem. Only in this way will realism be able to make good its claim to be a philosophy when confronted with the exclusivist pretensions of idealism, and it will also possess a criterion for criticizing and limiting itself without running the risk of falling into skepticism."[4] We are dealing once again with a realism that thinks it must be critical in order to be philosophical, and we will encounter the same problems expressed

[3] Ibid., 10.
[4] Ibid., 11.

in familiar terminology: a realism must necessarily either be critical, philosophical and reflective or else be a form of common sense, infraphilosophic and naive. In short, the possibility of a philosophical and reflective, yet noncritical, realism is not even considered.

But that is precisely the issue we wish to discuss, and denying or ignoring its possibility will require all the subtleties of critical realism, as we shall see. The positions between which we are asked to choose present a false choice because they both exclude without discussion one of the possible approaches to the problem of knowledge. This is why the reader may get the feeling that he is watching a dialectic constantly striving to refute positions that nobody holds. If absolute dogmatists contend that there simply is no problem concerning the validity of knowledge, they reply that there are numerous philosophers for whom there is a problem of knowledge. But this response is irrelevant from the point of view of one who maintains that a realist philosophy is unable to pose the critical problem of knowledge.

It goes without saying that every philosophy can and must come to grips with the problem of knowledge, as Plato, Aristotle, St. Thomas and many other medieval thinkers actually did. As St. Thomas said, the problem of truth arises from metaphysics and is therefore a problem. Everyone agrees that idealists may pose the problem according to the plan of the critique. What we wish to know is whether a realist philosophy is able to carry out a critique of knowledge, and that is an entirely different question. Realism will be quite able to defend its rights against idealism if it is philosophical. How, then, can realism also be expected to be critical, unless philosophy and the critique are identified? Thus, what was supposed to have been proven was a foregone conclusion from the very start.[5]

Once we have made these reservations it is only fair to follow Fr. Picard's efforts and watch his critical realism in action. After all it would be poor manners not to, for the process is neither long nor difficult to follow. "In all our psychological states we grasp, beyond any possibility of doubt and by means of a concrete, concomitant reflection, the existing self and the fact of its self-consciousness. This immediate knowledge of the self is not of the purely empirical order but is absolute. It is an experience that reveals to us the very reality of the self, not just its appearance, and at the same time it assures us of the essential reliability of our mind."[6] Obviously this critical philosophy will not shrink from dogmatic statements, but we must try to see what its essential elements are.

First of all, it is supported by a personal experience: the experience of the self and the contents of consciousness. This experience presupposes a reflection of the thinking self upon itself, but it is a concrete reflection because it bears upon an observable fact: the reality of the thinking subject, not some abstract concept like "thought in general" or even

[5] It is more difficult to characterize the analogous effort of R. Jolivet, *Le Thomisme et la critique de la connaissance* (Paris: Desclée de Brouwer, 1933). I must frankly admit that I am unable to understand the author's objection. After observing that I have often insisted that it was Descartes' infatuation with mathematical method that gave rise to and served as a foundation for his idealism (12), Jolivet declares that he cannot agree with me that the *cogito*, as such, is the source of idealism (19). How could I have held both positions at the same time? I have never ceased to state and explain that, once he had decided to proceed, like mathematicians, from thought to being, Descartes could find only one starting point for metaphysics: the *cogito*.

[6] G. Picard, op. cit., 46.

"the self". This reflection, therefore, leads to the apprehension of the existing self in its concrete reality which forms, with its actual conscious activity, "a living, objective 'something', positing itself absolutely, grasped as such".[7] In other words, we are dealing with an intuition and, although it may not grasp the truth distinctly and is perhaps more like touching than seeing, it is not simply an abstraction because it grasps an actual being directly. Such a knowledge is sufficient to overcome the universal doubt and assure us of the objective value of our knowledge, at least in the order of intuition.

But we can carry the analysis further still. From the fact that this immediate knowledge of the self attains absolute reality, not mere appearance, it follows that the "phenomenalism" we spoke of earlier is overcome at the same time as skepticism. But this is only thanks to the intuition of the self, for the only absolute which thought is able to attain directly is the thinking self. Thus, "it is *only to the extent that we have an intuition of the self that we have an intuition of being*, and this intuition of being, which has the same dual character of clarity and imprecision as the intuition of the self, puts us in possession of the absolute, justifies the evidence of the first principles and assures us of the essential trustworthiness of our minds."[8] Once assured of this first certainty it becomes easy to perform a critical deduction of the principles of knowledge, starting from the intuition of the existing self. The identity of being with being and its nonidentity with nonbeing immediately yields the principles of identity and contradiction. The dynamic self-sufficiency of being yields the principle of sufficient reason, not only as a fact but as a necessary law of being. Finally, whatever applies to the self,

[7] Ibid., 47.
[8] Ibid., 59.

insofar as it exists, must also apply universally to whatever else exists.[9]

Nothing could be more seductive than the easy and even somewhat cavalier way in which the validity of our knowledge is based upon a single metaphysical experience. It is hard not to admire the ease with which the whole chain of conclusions is derived from a single starting point, but matters become increasingly more obscure as soon as we stop to reflect upon just what has taken place. For the historically minded, what is most striking in an undertaking of this sort is its composite nature. What is actually taking place is a justification of the value of being, the first principle of Aristotle's philosophy, by means of the famous "I think, therefore I am", Descartes' first principle.

I am aware that certain philosophers disdain the history of philosophy, but many of them have paid dearly for neglecting this aspect of their education. We must ask whether or not the history of philosophy reveals certain necessary conceptual relationships which every dogmatic speculation, once it has been warned by history, is strictly bound to honor. Thus, from this point of view, the history of philosophy is far from being a mere string of anecdotes. Indeed, an aspiring philosopher who is ill informed as to the rules of the game he is playing will soon be led to mistake the most inevitable transformations of metaphysics for simple historical accidents, isolated from and independent of what came before.

Fr. Picard failed to perceive the paradoxical nature of his undertaking. Since he was seeking to justify a metaphysics of being by means of the Cartesian methodology, which had been designed to replace such a metaphysics, it was necessary

[9] Ibid., 66–67.

to ask why St. Thomas had felt no need to use this method. To the standard objection "St. Thomas never said that", Fr. Picard replies that, nevertheless, it is possible to find in his writings statements favorable to the Cartesian method. Moreover, St. Thomas' texts are not the exclusive source of true philosophy and, anyway, "Since St. Thomas never asked the fundamental critical question he naturally never answered it."[10] We, on the contrary, have posed the question and so must answer it, even if that entails saying something that St. Thomas never said.

This answer has much to recommend it, but still we must ask *why* St. Thomas never asked the fundamental critical question. On this point Fr. Picard offers us a remarkably facile explanation, worthy of the most simplistic historicism. The reason the scholastics did not consider these questions, he tells us, is because they were not "led by circumstances"[11] to do so. This is euphemism at its best. In place of "circumstances" we may insert: "Descartes and mathematics, and Kant and the mathematical physics of Newton". But that is not the real question. It is not even a question of knowing whether Aristotelian realism was a truth suspended in midair until the day that Fr. Picard correctly saw that the Cartesian principle, designed to destroy Aristotelian realism, was actually the only means of saving it. What we want to know, the precise question, is whether Aristotelian realism can and must seek its ultimate justification in the intuition of the self. It is quite true that if Thomism never asked this question we cannot hope to find the answer in one of St. Thomas' texts, but perhaps there is a reason why St. Thomas did not ask this particular question. Therefore, we must remain deaf to the most pathetic appeals

[10] Ibid., 78.
[11] Ibid., 60, n. 1.

to sincerity, and we may ignore these appeals without for-
feiting our philosophical honor, because it is no lack of
sincerity to refuse to ask a question which makes no sense. If
a question makes no sense, it is impossible, and no one is required to do the impossible.[12]

As a matter of fact Fr. Picard's rhetorical exhortations are
a trap, and he was the first to fall into it. Whenever a realist

[12] The most serious and instructive effort to give this rhetoric of
sincerity some kind of philosophic weight has been made by R. Vernaux, "La Sincérité critique chez Descartes", in *Archives de philosophie*
(Paris: G. Beauchesne, 1937), 95–180. It is a remarkable article that proceeds surely to its conclusion. The very rigor of his thought leads Vernaux to claim that there can be a perfectly sincere critical philosophy,
but one: 1) which does not attempt to doubt; 2) which does not question
judgments of existence; 3) which makes its presuppositions explicit:
logic, reason, the concept of truth, science, method and acts of
knowledge; 4) which does not start from a simple *cogito* (I think) but
from a *cognosco* (I know); 5) which considers a reflexive analysis to be
necessary but not sufficient and adds an ontological analysis, charged
with seeking in the known object the principles necessary to explain its
intelligibility. It follows from this that the critique's proper task is to
link the analysis of the subject, which is a psychology, and the analysis of
the object, which is an ontology. "It may not be much, but that is all
there is" (180). To which we will only add that all this is true because it
rigorously excludes any trace of the critique from knowledge. It is a
reflexive analysis of all the conditions of knowledge which assumes as a
given all that is indeed a given, both in the analysis of the object and of
the subject. Thus, it is a complete theory of knowledge: a realist noetic
completed by an epistemology. And, as such, it is perfect. Moreover, if
it thus becomes possible to criticize individual instances of knowledge in
the name of a theory of knowledge in general, not for a moment will
knowledge itself have been criticized, for its reality, as well as the reality
of all its conditions, has been accepted without discussion before any
analysis. We will have cause to return to the idea of a critique of
knowledge. For the moment we will merely note that Vernaux, who is
the last person to whom we would pretend to teach the meaning of
"critique", does nothing more than retain the word while emptying it

urges us to address ourselves to the critical problem we may be excused if we ask him to set an example for us. The usual result is that in order to establish his credentials as a realist our philosopher assumes without discussion everything the critique puts in question, and in order to justify his pretensions to be critical he points to some idealist Scylla and Charybdis through which his realism will have to pass.

The example of Fr. Picard illustrates this general rule to perfection. At first his ambitions seem modest enough. Not only does he not place the validity of reason in any real doubt, but he does not even really doubt the validity of the various assertions put forward by common sense. All he proposes to do is to transform the certitudes of common sense into philosophical certitudes. All this is highly laudable, to be sure, but it need not involve a critical attitude, unless all pre-Cartesian speculation is reduced to the level of common sense and philosophy is said to begin with the *cogito*. We should note here that, although Fr. Picard intends to pose the fundamental critical problem, the reason he goes beyond St. Thomas is not in order to prove that our intellect is able to grasp being. He simply wants to determine in what instance we can be certain that our intellect does grasp being. Again, we must note that, up till now, no distinctively critical problem touching upon the validity of our knowledge has been raised. We knew in advance that it was possible to grasp an "in itself". Now the only problem

---

of all distinctive meaning. Therefore, we will allow him the word, if it will make him happy; no one has done more than he to illuminate the abuse of the term, since he makes it a condition for calling any realist theory of knowledge "critical" that its criticism be reduced to a link between two dogmatisms which had already been freed of the critique. All of which amounts to saying that the term "critical realism" is acceptable as long as it means nothing.

is to decide which instance of such knowledge is valid and which is not.

At least this should be the only problem, except for the fact that, since Fr. Picard is trying to play a Thomist and a Cartesian game at the same time, his thought suffers from a fundamental ambiguity. This ambiguity is a result of the different sense in which the word "principle" is used in authentic Thomist realism on the one hand and, on the other hand, in the version of realism which Descartes proposed. For St. Thomas as for Aristotle, the principle of identity is an absolute necessity of thought because identity is an intrinsic necessity of reality. For Descartes, however, this principle merely expresses an abstract and purely formal necessity of thought. As a result, this principle can be used as a fertile starting point in an empiricist realism of the Aristotelian sort because sense experience constantly nourishes and guides its concrete applications. This is impossible in a realism of the Cartesian sort, for no *a priori*, quasi-mathematical method can extract from an empty formula what is not contained in the formula. In other words, the concept of being and the principle of identity remain in Cartesianism as abstract principles and formal regulators of thought, but they cannot be principles in the sense of a "beginning" or "starting point". This is why, unlike Aristotelian realism, in which being is both first principle and starting point, in Descartes' realism, being is a principle but no longer a starting point. The Cartesian first principle is the first reality self-evidently knowable by means of the Cartesian method: thought, to which being is in turn added to give us a "thinking being". No abstract consideration of being would have yielded such results, for being is an empty formula for Descartes, and no meditation upon it will ever turn up anything of worth.

Here it becomes necessary to decide precisely what is to be done. "Our goal", writes Fr. Picard "[is] to establish philosophically the aptitude of the intellect for truth. . . ."[13] How should this be understood? Not, as we have seen, in the sense of an *a priori* justification of the aptitude of thought for knowledge, an absurd enterprise in which neither Fr. Picard, Descartes, nor Kant was ever engaged. If that were the objective of the critique, there never could have been a critical philosophy, be it idealist or realist. The critique would simply have been the *reductio ad absurdam* of skepticism, such as was carried out by Aristotle long ago. Fr. Picard's true goal is to establish that there is at least one instance in which the intellect grasps truth because there is at least one instance in which the intellect grasps being. In short, he is seeking to establish the aptitude of the intellect for truth, that is, to prove experimentally that it grasps being by demonstrating that there is a privileged instance in which the success of this undertaking cannot be questioned.

Nothing could be better, but in what sense is this undertaking critical? If we wish to remain within the bounds of realism, it will be necessary to proceed as Descartes did, following an idealist but non-critical method. I think, therefore I am a thinking being, or a being whose substance is simply to think. This is how Cartesianism proceeds and, since Hume and Kant, it has been reproached for doing so. In order to justify this substantialism of thought it is necessary to assume, as Fr. Picard does, a direct intuition of the thinking substance itself. Descartes provided a justification for this procedure, but that must not prevent us from asking whether St. Thomas would have rejected such an approach out of hand.

[13] G. Picard, op. cit., 44.

It is easy to see why those close to Fr. Picard have been actively engaged in attempting to prove that St. Thomas admitted a knowledge, or rather an experimental perception, of the soul by the soul itself.[14] It is essential that this be so if Thomism is to be founded upon the *cogito*.[15] No greater clarity will be achieved by grafting this second question onto the first. Suffice it to say that the problem is not new and that there are many categorical statements in St. Thomas which make it very difficult to believe that St. Thomas would ever have admitted a direct intuition, no matter how vague or confused, of the essence of the soul by the soul. His empirical attitude is opposed to such a position: "Ut scilicet

[14] B. Romeyer, "Notre science de l'esprit humain d'après Saint Thomas d'Aquin", in *Archives de Philosophie*, vol. 1, report 1 (Paris: G. Beauchesne, 1923), 32–55. Also: "Saint Thomas et notre connaissance de l'esprit humain", in *Archives de Philosophie*, vol. 6, report 2 (Paris: G. Beauchesne, 1928).

[15] So that our discussion will not be unduly weighed down, we will examine the "I am" of Fr. Picard in conjunction with Descartes' *cogito*. He himself invites us to do so. However, we must add that Fr. Picard claims to derive his support from St. Thomas, Maine de Biran and St. Augustine (op. cit., 67–75). The best discussion of these texts, which Fr. Picard uses in such summary fashion, would have used up much more space than it could possibly deserve. It is well known that we think St. Thomas, like virtually everyone else, admits the *cogito* to be self-evident but does not subordinate sensible intuition to it, which is precisely the issue here. As for St. Augustine, it is incontestable that he uses the *cogito* as a starting point for his metaphysical speculation and considers it a refutation of skepticism as a self-evident intuition of a spiritual reality; but although Augustinianism contains a critique, it is precisely this Platonic critique of sense knowledge against which St. Thomas reacted so vigorously. Yet Fr. Picard would associate him with that same critique. No matter what other reasons Fr. Picard may have for advancing these two authorities, it is clear that, had Descartes' *cogito* never existed, no one would bother to search their writings for a solution to a problem which, everyone admits, was never raised by them.

per objecta cognoscamus actus, et per actus potentias, et per potentias essentiam animae; si autem directe essentiam suam cognosceret anima per seipsam, esset contrarius ordo servandus in animae cognitione."[16] And again: "Mens nostra non potest seipsam intelligere ita quod seipsam immediate apprehendat."[17]

If, as it certainly seems, these texts affirm that an immediate intuition of the thinking subject is impossible, then we must conclude that, far from introducing a critical problem into Thomism by founding it upon a direct intuition of the thinking being, such a position would in reality eliminate from Thomism those elements which render such an intuition impossible. To speak more precisely, this position would substitute a pseudo-Thomist dogmatism for a Cartesian dogmatism without becoming any more critical. We must note, however, that Thomist realism has been irremediably compromised in the process, and it is here that the inevitable second act of this little comedy begins to unfold. We have just seen that there is nothing critical about a doctrine that simply assumes without discussion that there is an intuition of the absolute being of the thinking subject. For lack of criticism an idealist method has been introduced into Thomist realism, an *ordo contrarius* to its essence which will destroy realism under the pretext of justifying it.

St. Thomas considers the existence of the external world to be self-evident and so feels no need to make use of the *cogito*. Not that he does not consider the *cogito* to be self-evident, but it is not the condition for our certitude that the external world exists. Descartes, on the other hand, does not consider the existence of the external world to be self-evident; thus he starts from the only self-evident judgment

---

[16] Thomas Aquinas, *De Anima*, bk. 2, lect. 6, Pirotta ed., n. 308.
[17] Thomas Aquinas, *Quaest. disp. de veritate*, q. 10, a. 8, resp.

of existence that remains: I think, therefore I am. As a result these doctrines develop differently, but their developmental patterns are in conformity with their respective essences and, since the doctrines are opposed to each other, so are their developments. The brute empirical fact that St. Thomas and Descartes followed contrary methods would of itself teach us nothing, but certain concrete metaphysical necessities follow, and this one first of all: the only possible reason for choosing the *cogito* as the starting point for philosophy is that some privileged self-evidence is attributed to it. This is how Descartes understood it, but, since this understanding of the *cogito* is contrary to Thomist realism, it must follow that the attempt to reach St. Thomas' conclusions while using Descartes' method is a self-contradictory undertaking.

Nothing could save Fr. Picard from the inevitable consequences of his principles. The pages in which he manipulates texts from St. Thomas and other scholastic doctors in an attempt to resolve a problem which "did not exist for them" do not, properly speaking, reach the level of either philosophy or of history. Those pages accomplish nothing less than the negation of the clear meaning of the texts, for it is impossible simply to insert a Cartesian method into the vacant space left by the absence of the critical problem in the writings of these doctors. If his effort were to succeed, it would first require the destruction of all their positive achievements. Nothing is more instructive than Fr. Picard's illusions in this regard. With the most perfect naiveté he sincerely believed that the scholastics never took the trouble to justify their principles by reflecting upon their source, "or as we say nowadays, by making the deduction".[18] However,

[18] G. Picard, op. cit., 60, n. 1.

the scholastics did do so, the only difference being that they started with being as their first principle rather than the *cogito*.[19]

Once the *cogito* is introduced into their realism it becomes necessary to justify the privilege which is accorded it, and this can only be done by downgrading the value of sensible knowledge in favor of some more or less Cartesian intellectual intuition. Far from filling some lacuna in Aristotelian realism, this negates its very essence. Now, Fr. Picard must have reached that point when he wrote, in an authentically Cartesian sense:

> Unlike sensible intuition, which is merely empirical in the worst sense of the word and which, as a result, even while imposing itself upon sensibility remains exposed to that doubt which is able to bend the intellect to its absolute value (or, in other words, is able to assert its right to unqualified assent), this grasp of being in the consciousness of the ego victoriously resists all attempts at doubt as long as it follows the intuitive approach. It is an encounter with the intellect, a metaphysical experience.[20]

Nothing could be more clear, and from this point on we may be sure of where we are, but it follows immediately that sensible intuition alone can never assure us of the existence of its object. Now, it is possible to maintain with Descartes that the *cogito* is needed to guarantee fully the existence of the external world, but it is impossible to do this in the name of an Aristotelian or Thomist realism in which the validity of sense knowledge is unconditionally accepted. If

[19] "Naturaliter igitur intellectus noster cognoscit ens et ea quae sunt per se entis in quantum hujusmodi; in qua cognitione fundatur primorum principiorum notitia, ut non esse simul affirmare et negare, et alia hujusmodi" (Thomas Aquinas, *Summa Contra Gentiles,* bk. 2, chap. 83).
[20] G. Picard, op. cit., 59–60.

sense experience is not self-evidently valid and fully sufficient in itself, if, left on its own, it must needs remain under
the cloud of a doubt that can only be lifted by the intellectual evidence of the *cogito*, then a breach has been opened
through which the whole of Cartesianism may pass. For it
would then be true to say, with Descartes, that the soul is
more clearly known than the body, and it would therefore
be necessary, on the basis of this privileged evidence of
thought, to construct the whole structure of knowledge
according to an order opposite to the one followed by medieval realism. Therefore, it is the Cartesian proof of the existence of God which is valid, since it starts with thought,
and it is also by means of thought that we must prove the
existence of the external world.

But the most extraordinary feature of this strange mix-
ture of St. Thomas and Descartes is the fact that the existence of the external world, cast into suspicion by
Descartes, is admitted with as little difficulty as in the doctrine of St. Thomas. Descartes was more logical in this
regard. Since he considered sensible intuition to be of doubtful value he undertook to prove the existence of its object.
Fr. Picard, on the other hand, seems to find it natural that
the metaphysical experience of the *cogito*, since it suffices to
guarantee the existence of its own object, should also serve
to guarantee the existence of sensible intuition's proper object. But there is no connection between the two instances.
The metaphysical experience of the existence of the thinking being may suffice to guarantee the ability of knowledge
to grasp the real and know it as it is, but it certainly does
not authorize us to posit as equally valid a totally different
type of intuition. I am, therefore X exists, is not a valid
inference. In other words, from the fact that thought
knows itself to be competent to grasp being, which fact is

grasped in its direct apprehension of the thinking being, it follows that if it were to grasp another type of being, it would be competent to know it also, but it certainly does not follow that it *does* apprehend another type of being, nor that the other type of being exists. The existence of the external world cannot be, for us, the object of a pure intellectual intuition; therefore, if sense experience does not guarantee that it exists, it must be proven. This is what Descartes had to do and tried to do; St. Thomas did not do it because he did not have to; but Fr. Picard had to do it yet did not seem to realize it.

The balance sheet for this metaphysical undertaking is not terribly impressive. But how could it be, since it is self-contradictory in principle? Therefore, one must be excused for expressing surprise at its numerous imitators among those who make a profession of interpreting medieval realism for the benefit of modern philosophers.[21] A fundamental critical problem which is discussed without even defining the concept of a critique, a realism in which what was obvious for realism became an idealist problem, although the conclusions drawn are neither obvious as they were for realism nor proven as they were for idealism: this is what is offered to our contemporaries to lead them to the eternal truths of metaphysics. Anything can happen, as witness Fr. Picard's new disciples, but philosophy itself will have gained nothing from it.

[21] See for example, P. Descoqs, *Institutiones Metaphysicae Generalis* (Paris: G. Beauchesne, 1925), 1:60–66. The author declares himself to be in full agreement with Fr. Picard and graciously excuses St. Thomas in the same way as Fr. Picard had done: "Non negamus momentum hujus facti S. Thomam partim latuisse, cum problema criticum tunc temporis non moveretur" (61).

CHAPTER FOUR

THE REALISM OF THE "I THINK"

Paulo majora canamus! Among recent attempts to construct a critical realism, Fr. Roland-Gosselin's must occupy the place of honor. Some may be more ambitious, but his is the most sincere, for its author does not play word games; he will not be satisfied with the mere appearance of success. Yet such is the nature of this problem that the very manner in which it is approached determines the outcome. Fr. Roland-Gosselin wrote the first ten pages of his book freely and under no constraint, then struggled through the rest of the book trying to avoid the consequences of what he had written in those first pages. But the battle was lost before it even began; without even realizing it, he had already laid down his arms.

Therefore, we must carefully scrutinize the first moments of the undertaking in which so much is decided. "Man may be considered as a part of the whole universe, and the various means by which he gains knowledge classified as so many aspects or principles of human activity."[1] Absolutely

[1] M.-D. Roland-Gosselin, O.P., *Essai d'une étude critique de la connaissance*, Bibliotheque thomiste 17 (Paris: J. Vrin, 1932), vol. 1: *Introduction and first part*, 9. This is the first sentence of the introduction. Cf. J. Jacques, "La Methode de l'épistémologie et l'essai critique du P. Roland-Gosselin", in *Revue neoscolastique de philosophie* 40 (1937): 412–40.

true. An assortment of different but interrelated beings engaged in certain activities; among these beings, man; among the activities in which he is engaged, knowledge; the theory of knowledge has as its object the reflective study of this most human of activities. There is nothing to criticize in such a position.

But we must pursue the discussion, for in the following lines Fr. Roland-Gosselin changes his field of operations to a much more restricted space, and when he finds himself trapped he considers it inevitable that we too should be entrapped with him:

> The least reflection upon the peculiar position occupied by knowledge in the life of man, and more especially in the speculative life (that is, philosophy and the more disinterested of the sciences), leads inexorably to the conclusion that the study of knowledge cannot be just one science among others, precisely because the object of such a study is so different from the objects of other sciences. Its object is knowledge itself. But knowledge is the means by which we attain every other object.[2]

It would be impossible to express better, if not the modern manner of conceptualizing the problem, at least the modern attitude toward the problem. Schools today are conducted in an atmosphere so saturated with idealism that a realist position has become almost inconceivable. Nowhere is this more true than in discussions dealing with the problem of knowledge. Indeed, it may be truly said that from the very beginning Fr. Roland-Gosselin excluded any possibility of a realist solution to the problem. We were in agreement with his picture of man and his ways of knowing as members of a universe of which they are only parts.

---

[2] M.-D. Roland-Gosselin, op. cit., 9.

Nothing could be more obvious, and this is the authentically realist way of presenting the question. Having received his place among the larger community of beings, man and the world are seen to be interrelated, and knowledge, conceived as an operation of that part of the universe which is man, is no less interrelated with man and the world. Although it is true that knowledge is the means by which we attain every other object of knowledge, it in no way follows that knowledge is not one object among many or that its study cannot simply be one science among many sciences. At least such a conclusion does not follow unless the problem of knowledge is presented as already resolved in an idealist sense. For it is first necessary to know what we are talking about when we posit knowledge as an object.

When do we encounter knowledge apart from a knowing subject? Doubtless some will say that the knowing subject grasps itself only as an object of knowledge, but that is not true, at least, once again, as long as the discussion is not cut short in favor of idealism. The simple truth is that the knowing subject grasps itself, by means of knowledge, as a subject distinct from knowledge itself. From this point of view there is no need to grant a unique privilege to knowledge and the science of which it is the object. It is certainly true that if man were not endowed with the power of knowledge there would be no object of knowledge, but it is equally true that if no object were given there would be no knowledge. Here we are faced with an initial choice which it is impossible to avoid. On the one hand we can conceive of man as a being, capable of knowledge, among other beings. On the other hand we can abstract the power of knowledge from the real subject (man), then endow this abstraction with a separate reality and finally confer upon this function abstracted from its subject the extraordinary privilege of questioning both the existence of the subject whose function it is and the existence of the other beings without which the function could not be exercised. Every realist philosophy holds that the second choice is arbitrary and can only claim to be necessary at the price of one or more sophisms. Fr. Roland-Gosselin did not realize this; therefore, he could not help becoming involved in an idealist method. He abhorred the conclusions of this method so much that his only reason for writing was to refute them, yet he found it impossible to escape their toils.

From this point on, the conclusions flow forth with that necessity proper to metaphysical relationships. Let us posit, hypothetically, "knowledge" as the means of attaining every other object. It is clear that once this abstraction has been performed we will be totally cut off from reality for, in the first place, knowledge has been posited as a reality in itself and, since nothing exists for us except through it and in it, knowledge contains all the rest. There is therefore no reason to break outside the boundaries of this abstraction and no means of doing so. Here knowledge is made the condition for all other things. If, therefore, "thought should fail me the world would continue on its course, but I would know nothing concerning it, and I would have no interest in the world or myself. As far as I would be concerned nothing would exist anymore."[3] From which it follows, not that what no longer exists for me no longer exists at all, but that, according to the proper program of epistemology, "our conception of reality, as indeed our conception of science, inevitably depends upon our conception of knowledge in general, its nature, power and value."

This initial inversion of the realist position necessarily entails

---

[3] Ibid., 10.

an analogous inversion of the hierarchy of the sciences. When every question starts with being, the highest science is the science of being as being. Therefore, every true realism recognizes the unconditional primacy of metaphysics. But when every question starts with knowledge, metaphysics loses its absolute dominance and must delegate some of its powers to the critique. Let us proceed further. No matter how much one may hate to admit it, the idealist position implies the unconditional primacy of the critique over metaphysics, at least as far as method is concerned. This is why, after telling us that philosophy is like a circle and may be entered either through metaphysics or through the theory of knowledge, Fr. Roland-Gosselin admits that, while either of the two alternatives is psychologically possible, only one of the two is logically valid. "History testifies that the natural impulse of the intellect is to start with metaphysics", but although they were originally united, the critique, properly speaking, has become progressively more distinct from the theory of being. Far from seeing in this relatively recent development an indication of the artificial character of the critical problem, he concludes that it corresponds to a progress of the intellect. The critique is man's intellect reflecting upon itself in order to gain an immediate knowledge of itself. "Therefore, if the critical problem is accepted it will take *a logical precedence over metaphysics*, since it conducts an inquiry into *the possibility of science and of metaphysics itself*. The critique need not have recourse to metaphysics in order to reach the solution it seeks, for if it should do so it will not have justified the validity of knowledge by means of the intellect reflecting upon itself, nor will it have demonstrated the necessity of a science of being."[4]

---

[4] Ibid., 11.

The passages which we have just stressed could not be more clear, and it is immediately evident that they will undermine Thomism while claiming to "facilitate exact knowledge and maintain its vitality among our contemporaries".[5] By an inevitable development of his initial positions Fr. Roland-Gosselin has reached the point of justifying all knowledge, *including metaphysics*, by means of a single, unique science: the science of knowledge. If this science exists apart from metaphysics, it must ultimately become the judge of metaphysics: "The trust accorded to science and metaphysics while they are being established *always* gives way . . . after the most brilliant successes to a certain uneasiness which neither science nor metaphysics itself can relieve. Of what real value are these theories and superb constructions of the intellect?"[6] Who will not recognize here the same tone found in the first pages of the *Critique of Pure Reason*? The same question which Hume's works aroused in Kant's mind will now wake Fr. Roland-Gosselin from his dogmatic, Thomist slumber, and since the question is Kant's it will be difficult to avoid reaching Kant's conclusion. It is only natural that poor Hecuba should be persecuted by a disciple of Hume, but one could certainly understand it if she were to say: *Tu quoque* . . . , upon seeing her downfall brought about by a disciple of St. Thomas Aquinas.

It is not as if Fr. Roland-Gosselin were unaware of the unusual nature of his undertaking, but the *a priori* arguments with which he attempts to justify it are extremely disquieting. In the first place, it is impossible to read the first few pages of his book without receiving the impression that at the time he wrote them he thought he had solved the problem

[5] Ibid., intro. 7.
[6] Ibid., 12.

of critical realism. If he had not been absolutely convinced of this, Fr. Roland-Gosselin certainly would never have been so imprudent as to publish the first part of his work. Moreover, he himself tells us that the critical question which he poses will not lead him to downgrade reason or scorn philosophy: "We do not think — as will become sufficiently clear in the course of this work — that we have been trapped by that difficulty."[7] Now, quite to the contrary, we will see that the further he proceeds in his undertaking the more insurmountable the difficulties he had flattered himself that he would conquer, or perhaps even thought he had already conquered, seem to become. It was precisely the critical attitude which he demanded that gave rise to this insurmountable difficulty: is it possible, in deference to the rights of the critique, to subordinate the science of being to a higher discipline without renouncing the whole economy of Thomist realism which he had hoped to justify?

Once the question is presented in this manner critical realism can only fight a holding action. The relationship between the critique and metaphysics, we are told, is circular. If we start with a theory of the intellect and succeed in "establishing the possibility of knowing the laws of being in general, it will then be time to turn the light of metaphysics on the theory of the intellect. Therefore, we do not intend to deny the ultimate right of metaphysics to dominate the study of knowledge, although the first steps of a theory of knowledge must logically precede a theory of being. We have attempted to conduct such a study, *prescinding from all metaphysical presuppositions.*"[8]

Here we see Fr. Roland-Gosselin's express intentions, but what do they really mean? The Aristotelian hierarchy of

[7] Ibid., 15.
[8] Ibid., 12.

sciences places the science of being, metaphysics, at its summit. This science judges all the others because it is the science of first principles and first causes, and the absolutely first principle is being. The order of the sciences and the supreme judicial authority of metaphysics are therefore indissolubly linked to a realism of being which lies at the very heart of this philosophy. If the first principle is truly being, then the science of being must be the judge of all the others without itself being judged by any of them. But if there is a science distinct from metaphysics, a science which is not a science of being and which is logically prior to metaphysics, established without regard to metaphysics, and if this science is so completely independent that it judges metaphysics, then obviously that science will have the highest rank among the sciences. In short, the critique of knowledge dethrones metaphysics, which now exists only at the pleasure of the critique. And will the critique need to be justified? If the critique is able to justify metaphysics, "prescinding from all metaphysical presuppositions", it must not need metaphysics in order to be established. On the contrary, if it needed metaphysics in order to function validly it would be impossible for the critique to justify metaphysics "prescinding from all metaphysical suppositions". Therefore, a choice must be made. Two distinct sciences cannot simultaneously occupy the highest rung unless the relationship between metaphysics and the critique is not only circular, as we were told, but viciously circular.

Fr. Roland-Gosselin's general justification of his critical undertaking called for a general critique. We must now examine the manner in which it is carried out in order to see how impossible is its burden of explaining away all the innumerable difficulties blocking its path, of which none is ever definitively disposed. In reality, what is needed is a critical justification of realism, and this presupposes a critique which will remain independent of both realism and idealism. A question, says Fr. Roland-Gosselin, which seems no more difficult to resolve than the consideration of any other problem in which we seek to know if it can be resolved and by what means. But that is the precise difficulty, for this problem differs from all other problems in that it deals with the first principle. We are told we must adopt an attitude which does not prejudge the truth of either idealism or realism, but that is impossible. If being is the first principle, which, after all, is possible, *ens est quod primo cadit in intellectu*, any affirmation whatsoever will imply a realist position, deciding the question in favor of realism from the start. If, on the other hand, a distinct science can be established without positing being, then thought, not being, will be the first principle and the problem will be immediately resolved in favor of idealism. Either way, a definite position will have been taken.

Confronted with this fundamental difficulty, critical realism has only one course to follow if it is to avoid confessing itself to be stillborn, and that is to devise some artifice to postpone the moment of truth at which it will have to admit that critical realism is simply not viable. Realism inevitably provides that artifice, for it is universally true. The artifice boils down to finding an instance in which the intellect grasps, immediately, some one thing in itself which is not a thing distinct from the intellect. Actually, this is not only possible but quite legitimate. Since the intellect is engaged as a whole in each of its acts we can be sure in advance that an analysis of any given act will find the intellect present in its entirety, including its first principle, being. The critique of knowledge, thus conceived, will be prolonged for the duration of this analysis. It will certainly end in the justification of realism, at least as far as the one case in question, but when it comes time to pass on to other instances, how will that be done? That is the real difficulty.

Certainly, by starting with an object of thought in order to avoid favoring realism, Fr. Roland-Gosselin does not, *a priori*, deny the ability of thought to attain other beings in addition to itself. He leaves open, in principle, the possibility of a realism of sensible being, but he has become entangled with an idealist method, and only his ultimate intentions are realist. To the extent that he is not aware of having failed in this undertaking, in which Descartes himself did not succeed, he will be able to preserve the illusion that he still does not put himself in hock to idealism. True enough, Descartes' failure, considered simply as an empirical fact, proves nothing. One can still try, one can *always* try. Yet the obvious reason which made Descartes' failure inevitable is of more than merely empirical interest, for we are no longer dealing with a problem in the history of *a* philosophy, rather, we are concerned with the very nature of philosophy itself. What history shows us here is that a problem of this type is *essentially* insoluble. The nature of Fr. Roland-Gosselin's undertaking is such that it requires a certain method, the same one which Descartes was forced to use. We have already seen Monsignor Noël cautiously probe its beginning while waiting for Fr. G. Picard to become entangled in it, but it was the only way that remained open for Fr. Roland-Gosselin. The only difference was that his absolute philosophical sincerity would not allow him to be content with Descartes. Since he thought a critique was necessary he had to begin, and it was his honor that led him to begin with the *cogito* of Descartes as revised by Kant.

It is of the very essence of a critique of knowledge to be a reflection of thought upon thought. Therefore it must inevitably start with thought, and, in this very general sense, it requires the *cogito* as its first step. Fr. Picard had already stated this principle, but, by immediately accepting, with Descartes, a type of immediate intuition of the absolute being of the thinking subject, he had oversimplified matters. To say nothing of what St. Thomas would have thought, it is absolutely certain that Kant's critique formally denied that a direct intuition of a thing in itself is possible. Thus, Fr. Picard's critique neatly sidestepped what Kant considered the critical problem par excellence: does reason go beyond phenomena, even in the order of thought? It will be quite otherwise in the work of Fr. Roland-Gosselin, who never forgot the old saw: nothing ventured, nothing gained. Although he started with the *cogito*, he clearly saw that the thought from which a critique must take its beginning is not the thought of a thinking subject but that of a critique. Far from getting involved from the start with a metaphysics, which would be to presuppose metaphysics, a true critique only starts out from itself. "I seek. And at the moment my quest begins I can consider it as first in relation to every act which follows from it. It gives them their meaning."[9] Thus, the fear of realism is the beginning of wisdom, to such an extent that we will start with Descartes' *cogito* as revised by Hume and Kant. It is true that the *cogito* remains inevitable and the certitude of its existence undeniable, but "as act, not as substance".[10] In short, there is a quest, and, for the moment, that is all that may be said, for it would be going too far to conclude: the critique exists, therefore I am.

Steeped as he was in the best scholastic traditions, Fr. Roland-Gosselin was able to draw far more from this meager starting point than most in his position could have done. Like every other judgment, "the critique exists" implies the notion of being. It is therefore as good a starting

9 Ibid., 20.
10 Ibid., 16.

point as any for a reflexive analysis of knowledge insofar as it is knowledge. As a matter of fact it is better than most other starting points, since it is immediately evident: "Nullus potest cogitare se non esse cum assensu." If this judgment is true, it is knowledge. But, it may be asked, what is it knowledge of? It is a statement which unites, while contrasting, two terms: the subject and the object. If, therefore, as is the case here, knowledge is posited as an object, it follows inevitably that the act of knowing should be thought of as existing: what *is* the object of thought itself. After all, how can you ask what it is without presupposing that it exists?

Thus we are in immediate possession of being and are in a position to isolate the key role played by being as the beginning and end of true judgments. This amounts to deducing all other principles from being. Certainly that can be done, and Fr. Roland-Gosselin did it magisterially, but he did nothing else. That is why, having achieved the first part of his program, he realized that the second part still remained. How can the thought of the thinking subject, even if in possession of the subject's being, grasp the being of anything other than itself? The starting point of the method has not changed. It is always the reflexive method exerting itself upon the content of thought. The difficulty remains the same: to get reflexive thought to leap beyond itself and land gracefully in the middle of the world of existing beings. It helps to crouch before jumping, but in order to jump there must be something to push off against, and in this case there is no such firm foundation.

It is unfortunate that this attempt at a critical realism, which was carried out with such uncommon dedication and intellectual vigor, should have been interrupted by the death of its creator. Instead of the major work which Fr.

Roland-Gosselin had hoped to write, we have only a number of essays and notes, but all who have read them have, with their editors, considered them "as interesting as if they were the finished product". As a matter of fact, their unfinished state may be to our advantage, for since they permit us to watch a mind grappling with an insoluble problem, they assure us that every conceivable alternative has been tried, and tried in vain.

While addressing himself to the critical problem in the notes that would have formed the second part of his essay, Fr. Roland-Gosselin recalls the necessity of asking the critical question, for "not to accept it [the critical problem] is a sign of baseless dogmatism, refusing the intellect the knowledge of itself that would allow it to justify its own worth."[11] Let us note in passing that this apparent direct thrust to the heart of the matter actually misses the point entirely. No realist denies the intellect the power to justify its own worth, but those under the spell of idealism cannot conceive of any other than a critical justification. As a result, for them a refusal to accept the critical problem amounts to a denial of the only means of justifying the validity of our knowledge. We must take the idealists as they are. Now, from here on in, Fr. Roland-Gosselin presents the problem in terms which are more and more clearly idealist. After having justified the general power of thought to grasp being and know it as it is, he goes on to ask whether the being whose existence has been posited by the judgment of perception may be posited by thought as really existent. In other words, once the validity of thought and the principles of thought have been established in the case in which the really existing being known by the intellect is the thinking

[11] M.-D. Roland-Gosselin, "Le Jugement de perception", in *Revue des sciences philosophiques et théologiques* 24 (1935): 13.

subject, it becomes necessary to establish the ability of each thinking subject to grasp beings other than itself, be they other thinking subjects or nonthinking subjects.

At the time he began this new inquiry, Fr. Roland-Gosselin felt sure that his hands were free. In reality, his hands were bound from the very beginning of his *Essai*. Why did he accept the idealist version of the problem? "Because", he tells us, "there is no need to yield meekly the privilege of a solid foundation, an unassailable starting point, to idealism. It may be possible to have such a starting point and acknowledge its natural offspring without being boxed into a corner."[12] Here we have one of those all too frequent cases of one who desires to be a realist deliberately painting himself into an idealist corner, all the while betting that he will find a way out. It is possible to approach the problem in this manner, but those who prefer the idealist statement of the problem undoubtedly consider it solid and unassailable, and so by the same token they must consider that the realist position is not, or is less, secure. From this it follows that, to their minds, idealism is the only absolutely unassailable form of the problem of knowledge. It is possible to hold this position, but it is then useless to pretend that your hands are still free, for you have agreed to do battle on the enemy's home ground and have allowed him the choice of weapons. Methodologically, at least, it is impossible to be neutral when you have committed yourself in either direction.

Thus, we are condemned with Descartes to search the content of our representations for something that will justify the actual existence of their objects. This content has a double aspect. One part is concerned with sensibility and

---

[12] M.-D. Roland-Gosselin, *Essai d'une étude critique de la connaissance*, 35.

THE REALISM OF THE "I THINK"

the other with the understanding. At first glance it is tempting to be content with saying that sensation allows us to attain real existence. But, as Fr. Roland-Gosselin recalls, "the senses do not perceive being or existence as such; they simply perceive the sensible, and primarily what is proper to the powers of the particular sense. What is called sensible per accidens (being, for example) is not, in reality, perceived by the sense itself. It is an object perceived by another faculty in conjunction with sensation, which would be the intellect where existence is concerned." Shall we now say that the intellect apprehends existence in perceptual judgments? That is equally impossible, for "the intellect has an immediate knowledge only of essence and cannot know actual existence."[13] It will not be easy to discover a solution to this problem.

To be sure, there was one solution: the inference used by Descartes and Cardinal Mercier. But Fr. Roland-Gosselin wanted to discover the external world, using the judgment, by analyzing the content of perception in the light of the first principles. He recalls the list of first principles, omitting the principle of causality, the use of which would transform this analysis into a synthesis. Having thus strictly limited the scope of his operations, he found that the only choice left was to compare the content of perception with the first principles in the hope of finding, without using an inference, something to which we are able to analytically affirm that a real being corresponds.

It is obvious from the start that such an undertaking will run into extraordinary difficulties, for it is an attempt to justify realism by using a method that is the exact opposite of its own. Left to follow his own inclinations, a realist

[13] M.-D. Roland-Gosselin, "Le Jugement de perception", 9; cf. 13.

would classify the contents of perception by comparing them to their real objects, and the first classification arises from whether or not there is a corresponding real object. The idealist, on the other hand, having nothing at his disposal but the contents of his perceptual judgments, must decide from the appearance of the contents of perception whether or not they correspond to some real object. For example: I see my typewriter. Therefore, you will say, since you see it, it exists. The inference would be valid if perceptions alone gave rise to existential judgments. Unfortunately, that is not the case, since there are many types of images or groups of images which are identical to perceptions in this regard. First of all, there are hallucinations which present themselves to the consciousness as if they were perceptions, although they are not. Dreams also are accompanied by a sense of existence no less acute than hallucinations. Moreover, all sense illusions, such as the stick which appears to be bent when thrust into the water, may be classed among those cases in which a simple image is mistaken for a perception. In short, in all these cases "the content of these images is spontaneously judged to exist independently of the intellect."[14] How, then, can we tell if the object of a perceptual judgment exists or not?

Since it is possible to make an existential judgment without having a perception, it is evident that images are just as able to serve as a foundation for such judgments as sensations are. Inversely, since it is possible to make an existential judgment without an existing object, it is not the presence or absence of an object which gives these judgments their peculiar character. From whatever side the problem is approached the answer still comes out the same: there is no existential

[14] Ibid., 7.

index, that is to say, a sign the presence or absence of which infallibly attests to the presence or absence of an object. In other words, "No sensation, nor any ensemble of sensations, is able by means of its sensible content to provide the intellect with a telltale sign permitting it to discern the real being of an object to which the contents of these sensations belong and which are a manifestation of it."[15]

From this point on Fr. Roland-Gosselin, like the idealists, becomes embroiled in a position that is not only hopeless but truly unintelligible. Long before him Taine had sought in mental impressions an infallible means of distinguishing between sensations and images. Fr. Roland-Gosselin took up the same problem and concluded that there is no telltale sign by which they may be distinguished. If, on the one hand, we cannot distinguish them by the presence or absence of an object and if, on the other hand, our sensations are not intrinsically distinguishable from our images, the question becomes not so much one of how we can solve the problem, but rather we must ask how we came to pose the problem in the first place. How, it may be asked, do dreams, illusions, reveries and hallucinations differ? But the very use of these words presupposes differences among these various states of consciousness, although we have been told that they are indistinguishable. If it is impossible to distinguish between a perception and a dream, why do we use two different words? Perhaps some will claim that it may be explained by conventions among men and that by crosschecking they have verified their experience. But we still do not know whether other thinking subjects exist. Or perhaps it may be explained by a reciprocal critique of our sensations among themselves. But if no sensation contains

[15] Ibid., 8.

an existential index, neither will a combination of sensations. The existence of the external world is not the only problem here. The existence of the problem itself is hard to explain.

In order to escape these difficulties, Fr. Roland-Gosselin tries several doors one after the other. The first is the one which leads to the old hypothesis of an active sense. But there is something paradoxical about attempting to clarify Thomism by introducing into it a doctrine which St. Thomas mentioned only in order to refute. For this undertaking to succeed, it would be necessary to show that St. Thomas was mistaken about the meaning of his own work. Such a hypothesis is not impossible, but its opposite is far more believable, and the discussion of this hypothesis demonstrates its complete hopelessness.

The hypothesis consists of assuming that there is, in sensations, in addition to the sensible species which is received, a species produced by the sense. This *species expressa* is conceived of as endowed with a specific intentionality which, like that of ideas, directs the mind toward reality. The only difference would be that, instead of directing the intellect toward being in general, as ideas do, perception directs it toward some particular being.[16] Aside from the difficulty of introducing an express sensible species into Thomism, this artifice fails because it is completely useless. If, as Fr. Roland-Gosselin himself has established, it is impossible to distinguish between sensations and illusions, then this express species, supposing that it exists, falls victim to the same difficulty. Whether or not there are such species, they could as easily be produced by a dream or hallucination. Therefore, the problem remains: "How can we establish, critically and

16 Ibid., 11–12.

with certainty, that a sensation or group of sensations is possible only by the action upon the mind of a reality which actually exists independent of the mind?"[17]

Since we have ruled out any recourse to the principle of causality, "which certainly plays no role in the spontaneous judgment of common sense", there is really nothing left to do but to trace the sensible data of perceptual judgment back to its existential judgment itself. Would it not be possible to analyze its spontaneous origin and, while tracing its origin, show how the contents of perceptual judgment imply realities distinct from the one who knows them? This is manifestly an appeal to psychology, but perhaps that is what is necessary to save metaphysics. One might say, for example, that an infant begins with a vague notion that its sensations or perceptions grasp really existing objects. Later on, thanks to the spontaneous application of the first principles and by comparing the different contents of perceptions, it becomes possible to apply the abstract notion of existence to certain perceptions. Once it is thus constituted, starting from certain sensible data, the idea of real existence can be immediately extended to each new content of sense perception. This extension is carried out so spontaneously that it soon goes beyond perceptions and embraces simple images also, thus giving rise to sense illusions, dreams and hallucinations. So, without any recourse to an intuition of being "which does not exist", we can understand how an existential judgment is formed. "Everything now takes on form and becomes coherent. All those formidable difficulties disappear."

But they do not disappear for long. The primary defect with this type of procedure is that it consists of inventing

17 Ibid., 13.

the desired response immediately after the problem is presented to psychology. It is too easy to dream up a psychology to fit the needs of a particular metaphysics. All that is needed is a little ingenuity, but this type of success has never proven anything. If we are to ask psychology to solve this problem we should leave it free to give its own response, only demanding that we not receive several contradictory answers, and we should submit to the conclusion reached, whatever it may be.

This field is hypothetical and uncertain, but even supposing that psychologists were able to give us a unanimous answer and confirm our realist expectations, what would we have accomplished as far as a critical justification of knowledge was concerned? Absolutely nothing. Common sense spontaneously affirms that normal perception attains real objects. Knowing by which psychological mechanism this conviction is formed gets us no further along the path of metaphysics than common sense had gotten us. It is useless to show how our perceptual judgments come to signify being, for that does not prove that perceptual judgments actually do attain being. To prove that, it is not enough to say that there are certain contents of perception which we must think of as really existing. The mere fact that we perceive sensible beings as existing leads to a pure empiricism, but the fact that we are constrained so to think does not get us beyond an abstract necessity which cannot guarantee the real existence of its object. Moreover, there is another point which our critical realist has not failed to notice. For, he observes, what we think of as a real object is often no more than an "objective unity", and we do not always know if it is also an "ontological unity". He immediately adds this disquieting remark: "But does this restriction not close off the road we have been following?"[18]

18 Ibid., 18.

It most assuredly does. As a matter of fact this road was closed from the moment we set out, but Fr. Roland-Gosselin does not yet lose heart in his lonely quest. After having analyzed the psychological formation of the objective unities of perception, he will seek to transcend psychologism by showing how "the object of perception must have the value of reality, independent of its unity. Is this possible?" And behold a new start: "It might be possible to think along these lines. . . ." The *Essai*, whose position we have already analyzed, has already proven the ability of the intellect to conceptualize being and to grasp it, starting from the experience of the "I think". Now, the concept of real existence only takes on its full meaning by means of sense perception. "Therefore, the concept of sensible existence thus acquired is valid in principle and truly possesses the meaning which the perceptual judgment spontaneously confers upon it."

Undoubtedly this is true, but in principle only. Now, the only reason we turn to this new argument is because it has already been proven that no image or perception can serve as an existential index. There are, therefore, two truths in conflict here. On the one hand, it is true that we spontaneously think of objective perceptual unities as corresponding to real beings; on the other hand, it is equally true that we are sometimes wrong to give in to this spontaneous urge, as in the case of a dream or a hallucination. How, then, are we to know when we are right? That is the whole question, and it will not go away. As Fr. Roland-Gosselin himself sadly confesses: "In principle, for it is obviously necessary to preserve the possibility of error. And that, perhaps, is the weakness of this demonstration."[19]

---

[19] Ibid., 20.

It may not be its weakness, but it is certainly its destruction. Unfortunately for us, this work was interrupted by its author's death and can tell us no more. After knocking at these different doors, all of which refused to open, this critical realist was forced into that time-honored activity of all prisoners: walking in circles. Sometimes Fr. Roland-Gosselin turns to the fact that since the intellect is known to be able to grasp being in the case of thought it must also be able to distinguish reality from appearance, even at the price of long, hard work. But then he remembers that it is a question of grasping a being in itself, not a simple necessity of thought and he realizes that he is right back where he started from.[20] Even if it is a necessary illusion, the existence of the external world is still just an illusion.

True, there are those who would say that if Fr. Roland-Gosselin had lived he would have found a way to fit the square peg into the round hole and construct a critical realism. We will not deny it, but we must be permitted to observe that Fr. Roland-Gosselin allowed himself to be carried along by the blind certitude that the idealist position was the only one which was truly solid and irrefutable. Since he had thus deliberately engaged in the public discussion of a problem for which he had not yet discovered a solution, he had to admit to himself that every method he thought up led in the end to the same impossibility. We know that this impossibility is coessential with critical realism. If you start with thought alone, you will never get beyond it, but if you do not start with thought alone, you will not have to do anything further in order to grasp existing beings since you will

[20] On the universal ability of the intellect to grasp being, see 22; on the time required to differentiate reality from appearance, 25, 27–28 and 35; on the difficulty of grasping something in itself, other than thought, 35–37.

already be in contact with them. Fr. Roland-Gosselin neither wanted simply to accept them nor was able to be re-united with them. It is possible to say without slighting his memory: where he failed, greater men had failed before him.

CHAPTER FIVE

THE REALIST CRITIQUE OF THE OBJECT

The task Fr. J. Maréchal set himself was twofold: first, to construct a theory of knowledge whose elements, while not fully articulated in the doctrine of St. Thomas, are scattered throughout his work, and then to apply the conclusions of this theory to "the solution of the fundamental problems of critical philosophy". This was the task he set himself, and he carried it out with remarkable power. Of course, the result could have been foreseen. It was an attempt to demonstrate that "Kantian agnosticism is not only not irrefutable; it can actually be overcome while starting from its own principles."[1]

The attempt was not unprecedented. Fichte had tried it, and the recollection of that powerful mind suffices to alert us to the fundamental difficulties involved. It is not impossible to vanquish the Kantian critique using its own principles, provided you interpret as metaphysical those terms which, in Kant's doctrine, are and seek to remain critical. Therefore, it will not suffice to object that Fr. Maréchal knew well enough not to try to resolve the problem in the same way Fichte did. Whether the critique is prolonged by a metaphysics of the subject, as in Fichte's case, or by a metaphysics of the object, which Fr. Maréchal attempted,

[1] *Le Point de départ de la métaphysique*, vol. 5, *Le Thomisme devant la philosophie critique* (Paris: F. Alcan, 1926), I.

the difficulty remains the same. Kantian critique is of its essence incapable of being extended into a dogmatic metaphysics, for the two are essentially incompatible positions, and any progression from the first to the second is treason. Kant said as much to Fichte often enough for his words to be remembered, and since we are here concerned not simply with critique in general but with Kantian critique, one must think twice before ignoring Kant's interdict on all such attempts. But let us at least give Fr. Maréchal his due: he faced this formidable obstacle conscientiously, for he had not forgotten Fichte. He foresaw that there would be those who would reproach him, as Kant reproached Fichte, for "pouring a whole metaphysics into the framework of the critique" at the risk of submerging the critique in metaphysics. As a result, he had an almost fraternal feeling for Fichte, for they were at antipodes and therefore in the same world, whereas Kant inhabited a totally different world. There is no other way to make sense of the remark with which Fr. Maréchal rejects this objection: "As far as that is concerned, we see no great difficulty. A critique need not necessarily preclude all metaphysics; a critique does not prejudge the absolute value of its object."[2]

Alas, that is just the question! As a matter of fact, Kant's critique does prejudge the absolute value of its object, so much so that it is essentially founded upon this very prejudgment, which the whole *Critique of Pure Reason* has as its end to justify. We may agree that this manner of presenting the problem is arbitrary, but that is not the question. The whole question here is whether it is possible to overcome Kantian agnosticism "starting from its own principles". To this we must answer: no, for Kantian agnosticism is inscribed

[2] Ibid., 5.

within the principles from which it flows, which is precisely why they are its principles. Therefore, if you engage in a critique that in no way prejudges its object you may be able to extricate yourself from Kantian agnosticism, but you will not have done so by starting with its own principles. It will be necessary to make a fresh start. If, however, you do indeed start from the principles of Kantian agnosticism, you will necessarily fall prey to the very agnosticism you were seeking to avoid.

It is easy to show that, from the start, Fr. Maréchal took his stand on ground that was completely foreign to Kantianism. If he had not, he never would have been able to advance a single step in his undertaking. In order to gain the freedom of movement he needed, Fr. Maréchal began by distinguishing two critiques. One, the "metaphysical critique", is a critique of the object. It presupposes not only that beings exist but also that every act of knowledge is naturally oriented toward being. Once this has been accepted the critique begins. It consists of returning to these initial affirmations by means of the reflexive method in order to criticize them. A whole series of problems then arises, all of which demand a solution. What conditions must be fulfilled, in regard to both the object and the subject, in order that knowledge may be possible? What are the different orders of knowledge and what are their relative positions? Finally, what are the degrees of being which correspond to the degrees of knowledge? Such a critique deserves to be called metaphysical for "it presents the object immediately as an object in itself", and only then, from this absolute perspective, does it analyze its object from without, according to the requirements of the principle of identity and without seeking the origin of the object in thought. Only later is the problem of the origin of the object of thought presented, and rational psychology determines the conditions on the part of the subject.

To this metaphysical critique is opposed the "transcendental critique" conceived of by Kant. Its essence consists of "suspending the primitive, absolute affirmation of being in order to examine the contents of consciousness in themselves and to analyze the conditions which constitute them as objects of knowledge". The problem which is presented is that of "the internal origin of the object as object". Its study, conducted entirely from within consciousness, far from presupposing any metaphysical affirmation, actually constitutes an "epistemology preliminary to metaphysics".[3] In order to construct a critical realism it is necessary and sufficient to cause these two critiques to coincide.

Like all problems, this one is condemned by its very nature to search for a solution in a predetermined direction. First of all, it is forbidden to limit in any way the claim of the so-called metaphysical critique to a total, objective grasp of being as it really is. The least restriction of this claim would have the immediate effect of destroying the metaphysical critique. Undoubtedly the subject plays a role in the constitution of the known object even in a metaphysical critique, but a metaphysical critique is forbidden to doubt the "objective absolute" grasped by knowledge. Nor is it permitted to doubt that, under conditions yet to be defined, knowledge truly grasps the known object. Since it is not possible to modify this type of critique, the only hope left is that the transcendental critique will prove more pliable. Is this possible? Dare we hope?

Not only did Fr. Maréchal hope and believe that this was possible, but his whole philosophical construction rests

---

[3] Ibid., 29–30.

upon this hope. If, as we fear, he was mistaken upon this point it certainly was not from ignorance of authentic Kantianism; on the contrary, his whole work proves that he had clearly discerned its spirit. More probably he failed to take critical idealism seriously. Actually, few critical realists really do engage in a critique; this is why they think it is so easy to escape it. However, like realism, the critique is controlled by the necessity of its essence, whose most fundamental requirement is that of identity and fidelity to itself. Even if the critique no longer knows what the first principle is, it is still governed by it. Whoever truly engages in the critique, rather than merely imitating it, quickly perceives its first law: it is essential for the critique to exclude all non-critical positions from every inquiry.

Fr. Maréchal violated this law from the beginning of his undertaking. In fact, the very formulation of this undertaking is self-contradictory from a critical standpoint. For let us not forget that this practitioner of a new type of critique retained a fully developed metaphysical realism which was explicitly exempted from all criticism. Not only did he not engage in a critique in the same sense as Kant did, although all other ways were closed to him, but he had already followed the course of metaphysical realism from beginning to end, and not a doubt had been raised in his mind concerning the perfect legitimacy of the results he had obtained. The problem that preoccupied him was to know if it were possible to attain the certitudes that realism had been able to assure, but by means of the critique. Such an undertaking implies a radical misconception of the uniqueness of pure philosophical principles and of the internal necessity which binds principles and conclusions. In reality, it is no more possible for a realist to pose the critical problem of knowledge than it is for a practitioner of the critique to embrace the conclusions of realism. Fr. Maréchal seems to have believed that a sufficiently clever metaphysical diplomacy would be able to induce the critique to renounce its very nature.

What confers a special interest on Fr. Maréchal's attempt is that, having played the part perfectly from beginning to end, he at least demonstrated that it is impossible to win at this game. From the outset he clearly saw that, unlike the metaphysical critique which first of all affirms the absolute reality of its object, the transcendental critique halts the movement of the intellect toward its object "and isolates the apparent content of consciousness in order to consider it in itself".[4] Moreover, Fr. Maréchal emphasized that in a transcendental critique the object is never defined as a function of the real object, supposing that there is one, but as a function of the faculties or powers of thought which constitute it as an object. That is precisely the transcendental point of view, in the Kantian sense of the word. It consists of viewing objects of knowledge strictly as a function of the faculties of thought that gave rise to them as objects of thought, which is to say: as objects, period, since unless it is an object of our thought it is not an object at all. Finally, we should add that Fr. Maréchal has denounced, with commendable vigor, the classic misinterpretation of these faculties as psychological entities. We stress this point because it indicates that this critical realism will reject any facile or dishonest solution. If the faculties of the critique were transformed into psychological entities, nothing would be easier than to reconcile Kantianism and Thomism, for the critique would then be limited to saying that there are ontological conditions of knowledge in the subject as well as in the object. But neither Aristotle's agent intellect

4 Ibid., 15-16.

nor St. Thomas' can be reduced to the status of mere *a priori* conditions of knowledge. They are causes because they first exist. Objectifying the Kantian faculties is a desertion of the critique's basic plan for that of dogmatic realism. The problem may be sidestepped by proceeding in this manner, but it will not have been solved. Fr. Maréchal really did want to resolve the problem. He very rightly remarks that "a faculty here is nothing more than an *a priori* power of determining the object."[5] Thus, just as the transcendental critique has nothing to do with what the object given to our senses is in itself, since in itself it is not an object, it likewise is not concerned with what the *a priori* determining conditions of the object are in themselves. It is necessary to have such determinants just as it is necessary to have things in themselves, but we know nothing of things in themselves except that they appear, and we know nothing of the *a priori* powers except that they set conditions. Not only do we know nothing more than we have indicated, but every question in this regard is without any meaning in the theoretical order. There is therefore no hope of overcoming the critique from this side. Fr. Maréchal saw clearly that the critique completely blocked all access to the subject or object in itself, and it is to his credit that he did not attempt a solution from this angle.

Having come this far, he did not hesitate any longer to set out on the difficult and deep path which leads through the very heart of Kantianism. Kant was convinced, against Hume, that there is universal and necessary knowledge concerning the real order. He was equally convinced that the reason Hume doubted the possibility of such knowledge could be found in the English philosopher's unconsciously

[5] Ibid., 16.

dogmatic conception of knowledge. At bottom, Hume's skepticism was the inevitable consequence of a doctrine in which the most simplistic empiricism claimed a knowledge of things in themselves. If the knowledge of things as they are in themselves is a self-contradictory undertaking, Hume's skepticism proved only (but this alone made it a decisive philosophical event) that all dogmatic knowledge is impossible. In other words, Hume's experience proved that every dogmatism engenders a fatal skepticism, but it did not prove that another type of knowledge is impossible. Let us suppose, therefore, with Kant, that we can go beyond the psychological empiricism of the subject to which Hume had been confined in order to raise ourselves to a pure, critical viewpoint. From this vantage point the problem appears in a different light. The problem now will be to discover which *a priori* conditions make necessary knowledge of objects possible.

There are two conditions. If necessary knowledge is not to be tautological and if it is to be a true enrichment of thought, it must be synthetic. Moreover, if these syntheses are not to be merely empirically consecutive but necessary laws, they must be *a priori*. Thus, the goal of the critique is to show that the existence of universal and necessary knowledge, Newtonian physics, for example, requires as a condition the power to form synthetic *a priori* judgments. This is not all. If the critique itself is to have necessary validity, it will not suffice to show that, in fact, our universal and necessary judgments are so constituted, for that would still be empiricism. It is necessary to prove that the very possibility of such judgments requires these principles. Since this is a "question of law" and not of fact, the demonstration must be analytical and deductive. It will consist of discovering in the objects of thought all the *a priori* conditions of their possibility. To carry out this analysis is to perform the transcendental deduction of the *a priori* conditions of thought by starting from these objects.[6] This is how the critique transcends all empiricism, both the psychological empiricism of the subject and the physical empiricism of the object. That there is universal and necessary knowledge is a pre-critical statement, as is the statement that beings exist. In the theoretical order the critique begins with the search for the *a priori* conditions of the possibility of such knowledge, and it is completed with their discovery. Once these *a priori* conditions have been discovered and identified as such we have said all that can be said concerning them. Speculation on the existence of things in themselves and the conditions of such existence finds itself relegated to the vague zone of dogmatic metaphysics, where reason discusses but never concludes.

The heroic task which Fr. Maréchal set for himself was to force the gates of the prison in which reason had been confined by the critique, and to do so from within. How can we proceed from the transcendental critique to metaphysics? Where can we find a way out that will lead from the pure *a priori* conditions of knowledge to the real being of objects? Fr. Maréchal sought this outlet in the fact that from the point of view of the Kantian transcendental analysis the object of knowledge is constituted by a faculty or, if you prefer, a power of joining, a synthesis, in short, an act of understanding. It does not much matter what name is given to this *Verstandeshandlung*; Kant himself used several names. What is important is that, for Kant, every object of thought presupposes the act from which it arises. We should add that this is one of the classic false doors through

6 Ibid., 22.

which the prisoners of Kantianism have sought to escape. To name only the most illustrious of them we need but recall Fichte. It is therefore true that by using this way in his turn Fr. Maréchal is engaging Kantianism upon one of the paths by which it is possible to escape. If there is an act of the knowing subject at the origin of every known object, there is necessarily a dynamism in every transcendental act of thought, and it is likewise necessary that this dynamism be oriented toward the constitution of the known object. Thus, finality is involved, at least on the epistemological level. "Kant misunderstood the essential role which the active finality of the subject plays in the very constitution of the immanent object, and this oversight robs his transcendental method of some of its power." Fichte, who realized this, rightly rebuked Kant for it, and, when he himself attempted to use this dynamism to unify the critiques of pure and practical reason, he was "not entirely wrong in believing", despite Kant's protests, that he was continuing the authentic work of the Kantian critique "by developing its implicit elements".[7] For if you adopt this approach it immediately becomes apparent that, far from being contradictory, the two critiques here in question, the metaphysical and the transcendental, converge toward the same end.

For the ancients, every judgment had objective value because it was an act of affirmation, and every affirmation implies a stable relationship between what is affirmed and being. Their realism, therefore, rested in the last analysis upon an implicit finalism of the act of judging, "which means in effect that the content of our knowledge always has some objective reality because, in one way or another, it is inevitably inserted into the absolute finality which animates

[7] Ibid., 26.

our action. The object is affirmed as *being* to the extent that it is necessary as an end."[8]

Once the object has been posited as an object in itself the whole thrust of the metaphysical critique will therefore be to turn back reflectively upon this affirmation and, in the light of the first principle, being, to describe and organize being according to the various levels and degrees of reality attributable to objects. The transcendental critique, on the other hand, can only start from objects of thought. If, however, rather than considering objects as static data, as Kant did, it returns to the dynamism of the act which constitutes the objects and to the conditions of this dynamism, it will be apparent that it is obliged to posit one end as its ultimate explanation. In other words, "the presence of the relative in consciousness leads to the discovery of the ontological absolute."[9] At this moment the two critiques are reunited in a single dynamic metaphysics which is their inevitable final result. If we go further we will see that they are implied in one another:

> Since both critical methods deal with the same subject matter from complementary points of view, they must ultimately yield identical results, if pursued to their logical conclusions, for the ancient critique simply posited the ontological object, which includes the transcendental subject, and the modern critique is concerned with the transcendental subject, which postulates the ontological object.[10]

The accord between the two critiques seems to be inscribed within their very essence, provided only that each of them be carried out thoroughly and, once completed, not be pursued any further.

[8] Ibid., 28.
[9] Ibid., 30.
[10] Ibid., 30–31.

This presentation of the two critiques as complementary aspects of a single undertaking is certainly seductive. It would be even more so if we were able to follow Fr. Maréchal through to its completion. But since our discussion is essentially concerned with method, we must deny ourselves this pleasure and, not without admiration for such a pretty reconciliation of ideas, mercilessly demand that he justify the general thesis advanced in the foregoing analysis.

Let us not forget that we started with the desire to arrive at Thomist realism by way of the Kantian critique. Now the method Fr. Maréchal recommends raises serious difficulties from a Thomist point of view. As a matter of fact, it raises insuperable barriers to a true union between the two critiques. Not only their union but their simple agreement appears to be impossible unless we strip each critique of its essential characteristics. It is true, although in a sense different from the one Fr. Maréchal employs, that the Thomist judgment implies an element of finality, but this very finality of Thomist "intentionality" presupposes, among other conditions, an already completed union between the subject and the object. It expresses the prior grasp of an "in itself" on the ontological level, the knowledge of which allows the knowing subject to be conscious. Thomist epistemology thus rests upon and is conditioned by an ontology which can be known and understood but need not be justified by epistemology. When thought turns toward an object, the object has already taken the first step. It is because the object has first come up against the subject that thought is then able to turn toward it. Moreover, this is why, unlike the transcendental critique, the so-called metaphysical critique has no need to postulate its object; if it had not already grasped this object, neither it nor its finality would exist.

On the other hand it is possible to say, if you wish, that the transcendental Kantian act implies a finality and postulates its object, but with what object are we concerned? If it is the immanent object of thought, we need not postulate it. It is already given as the very object of the transcendental analysis, but this is a mere object of thought, nothing more. In order to posit the thing in itself, the real being, as a condition of the finalism of the act of knowledge, it is necessary to be freed of all those operations which go far beyond the methods of the critique and whose results do not satisfy dogmatic realism anyway. There would be no difficulty in positing as possible the existence of the thing in itself. Kant himself never hesitated to affirm its existence, and here it would be enough to affirm its possibility. It would then be easy to show that nonintuitive thought like ours requires and posits, by the finality of its dynamism, "the independent reality of the ends it pursues". But, as Fr. Maréchal himself immediately adds, "from a strictly critical point of view a dynamic necessity, no matter how ineluctable, can of itself only be the basis for a subjective certitude."[11]

What resources does the Kantian method place at our disposal in order to objectify that certitude? Absolutely none. To get around this difficulty Fr. Maréchal quickly adds that, if one could show that the reality of the ends of thought is not only a dynamic necessity but also a logical necessity, the task would be successfully completed.[12] But this is not so, for, outside of relying unduly upon the data of the metaphysical critique, such a demonstration would lead only to an abstract necessity of thought which, no matter how absolute, does not guarantee the real existence of its

[11] Ibid., 334.
[12] Ibid., 335.

object. In short, critical thought has imprisoned itself and can find no way to be reunited with reality.

It is hard to believe that a philosopher of Fr. Maréchal's caliber did not perceive the radical inability of his transcendental critique to transcend itself and rejoin the order of existence. Since he persisted in this undertaking in spite of the frustration to which he was apparently condemned, he must have expected less in the way of results than is commonly thought. Having started with an object of thought he ended up with an object of thought, yet he seems to have considered the process worthwhile simply because it concludes with the statement that the object of thought whose postulation is logically necessary for the transcendental critique coincides with the absolute object whose real existence is affirmed by the metaphysical critique.

If, as we think, Fr. Maréchal's critical realism intends no more, it becomes clear that all we can expect, if it should succeed, is a proof of the agreement between the two critiques[13] but not a justification of the conclusions reached by the one while starting from the principles of the other. Perhaps a better way of putting it would be that two systems of ideas have been set up such that for every element of one there is a corresponding element in the other. They correspond exactly, like points on two parallel lines that never meet, for the transcendental critique eternally postulates an "in itself" without ever attaining it, while the so-called metaphysical critique, possessed from the beginning of the "in itself" of its object, always attains it without ever having had to postulate it. The transcendental critique will simply have proven its inability to attain the reality which it refused to accept.

13 Ibid., 32.

Still, in order to get these meager results it is necessary to have a particularly accommodating transcendental critique: in a word, Kant's critique as domesticated by Fr. Maréchal. We have noted with what honesty the author of this new critique adheres to the transcendental program, but he loses his engaging honesty by duplicating this program with a parallel metaphysical program in which permanent contact with the "in itself" is retained. Now, the transcendental critique does not simply disagree with such contact; it rejects and excludes it as contrary to the very nature of the critique. To seek not merely union with but duplication of a transcendental critique of the subject from a metaphysics is to seek to establish a correspondence between the critique and its very opposite. It is not true to say that the transcendental method of analysis is only meant to clarify.[14] It is exclusive, and that not by accident due to some misunderstanding on the part of Kant, but of its very essence. Even when it postulates the existence of the ontological object as being that which it determines as an object of knowledge, this ontological object *and its very postulation* remain completely outside the critique, for it is of the essence of the critique to cast a blanket, preliminary exclusion over the ontological object. The critical consideration of a real object would be the knowledge of an "in itself" from the point of view of the transcendental conditions of its knowledge, which would be to view the "in itself" as existing *only as an object of thought*. Every transcendental critique conceived of as a commentary on a metaphysics will therefore begin by denying the right of metaphysics to exist. It cannot justify metaphysics, it can only replace it.

It is true that the abstract character of the opposition

[14] Ibid.

between metaphysical realism and the transcendental critique makes it difficult to perceive. However, it is precisely this that gives it its pure formal necessity. The factual impossibilities which arise when the two orders are mixed are only the external signs of the initial confusion from which they flow. Every critical realism involves similar impossibilities, and, although each variety has its own favorites, their cause is the same. In Fr. Maréchal's case the confrontation of Thomism with critical philosophy leads to consequences as dangerous for Thomism as they are unacceptable for the critique.

When he attempts to transpose Thomist Aristotelianism in terms of the transcendental critique, Fr. Maréchal is confronted with serious difficulties, the greatest of which is to deduce "noumenal reality as a speculative necessity". Let us start with him from the fact that human intelligence is discursive and therefore implies a dynamism. Let us also admit that "every movement tends toward a final end according to a law or specifying form and the dynamic mark of the final end leaves its imprint on each stage of the movement."[15] Finally, let us concede that the objective final end, the *a priori* specifying form which orients our intellectual dynamism, can only be the absolute Being, God.[16] There is nothing in such an *a priori* deduction which is not in agreement with Thomist metaphysics. Undoubtedly, the exact nature of the implicit affirmation of God which such a doctrine presupposes must be made more precise, but the thesis is susceptible of a perfectly correct Thomist interpretation, which suffices for our present purposes. The real difficulty

[15] Ibid., 415.
[16] Ibid., 424. Moreover, this is why, in Fr. Maréchal's doctrine, the proof for God by means of efficient causality (which is the Thomist proof par excellence) becomes a correlative of the proof from finality. Cf. 425.

lies in the fundamental incompatibility between the Thomist transcendental critique and Kant's method, and in the impossibility of bending Thomism to meet the demands of such a method. Actually, it is apparent from beginning to end that this transcendental deduction has a metaphysical nature. Therefore, it is not critical at all, and Kant has every right to consider it null and void as a transcendental critical deduction. To establish a final end of discursive knowledge and to identify it with absolute being is the epitome of those operations which the Kantian critique condemns as illegitimate because they consist of turning simple *a priori* conditions of knowledge into hypothetical beings. Between the transcendental *abstracted from experience* by Thomist realism and the transcendental *condition of experience* is an unbridgeable gulf. One position is conceivable only because it presupposes being, the other determines the *a priori* conditions of the possibility of conceiving being. One is present at the heart of noumenal reality, the other is forbidden any access to noumenal reality because the conditioned and the unconditioned are mutually exclusive. The transmutation of Thomism on the plan of transcendental metaphysics will therefore not have the effect of disarming the critique; every undertaking remains faithful to its essence, which it cannot renounce without losing its own identity.

It is unfortunately inevitable that if you reconcile the irreconcilable, you will instead compromise what you had hoped to reconcile. Thomism's transcendental deduction is not a critical deduction, and the simple fact that it is *a priori* suffices to destroy its Thomist character. Like every realism, Thomism proceeds either from one reality which is empirically given to another reality which is empirically given or from one reality which is empirically given to another which is not but whose existence it is necessary to posit because of the absolute value of the first principles of reason. In both cases reason is directed toward a sensible datum in which an actual existent is immediately given. Therefore, in a metaphysical realism of this type absolute being may be posited only because there has been a prior sensible grasp of a real being. In short, the proof for the existence of absolute being is necessarily *a posteriori*.

In order to deduce noumenal reality as a speculative necessity it is necessary to reverse this order. Rather than being posited as the conclusion of a reasoning process which began with the grasp of being in experience, absolute being becomes the necessary *a priori* condition starting from which sensible experience itself is required. From this, Fr. Maréchal's fourth proposition is derived: "A discursive (nonintuitive) knowing faculty, constrained to pursue its end by successive movements from potentiality to act, can only do so by assimilating a foreign datum. Therefore, the exercise of our intelligence requires an associated sensibility."[17]

A strange Thomism indeed, which is compelled to justify the necessity of the sensible order, an order which Kant himself accepted but which Fichte believed had to be deduced. Actually, the introduction of "an extrinsic datum under the absolute finality of the rational subject"[18] is no less impossible for a transcendental critique than for a metaphysical realism. Critically speaking it is an idealist deduction of sensibility which, although permitted by Fichte's metaphysics, is not permitted by the Kantian critique. Thomistically speaking it is a subordination of the realist order of ends given in sensibility in favor of the idealist order of ends

[17] Ibid., 411.
[18] Ibid., 413.

required by thought. Thus, sensibility is required by the absolute end whose existence it will later prove. In other words, whereas in Thomism the existence of sensibility alone permits us to attain the existence of God, both as final and efficient cause, in Fr. Maréchal's doctrine it is the existence of God which permits us to attain sensibility. There is more and worse to come, for in a doctrine of this sort, God, or absolute being, cannot be truly proven to be the final cause.

In order to follow Kant's procedure we decided to start only from objects of thought, from which we went back to the act that constituted these objects, then to the dynamic orientation of this act and to the absolute end which this dynamism postulates. God is therefore no more than a postulate whose logical necessity does not guarantee his real existence. As for sensibility, it is a postulate of a postulate, and its existence becomes still more problematical. Having sought to deduce being from thought, although being is encountered first, the very being encountered is rendered problematical. In other words, the necessary characteristics of real objects from which metaphysics draws its nourishment have been reduced to so many necessary characteristics of objects of thought which the critique labors over. Thomism does not require God as a postulate; it posits him as a cause. Thomism does not postulate sensibility as a function of our knowledge of God; it accepts sensibility as a fact which becomes the means for our knowledge of God. This order, essential to metaphysical realism, is ruined if it is inverted.

There is nothing to prevent anyone who wishes from making an attempt of this sort again. It is not likely that many who renew the struggle will do as well as Fr. Maréchal did, but, no matter how they are carried out, all such attempts will end up with the same negative results. The very idea of deriving a metaphysics from the critique is self-contradictory and, critically speaking, impossible. Whoever becomes involved in this undertaking, as Fichte and Fr. Maréchal did, betrays the critique. Nothing better reveals the heart of the problem than this simple question which Fr. Maréchal asked himself: "Moreover, can a critical philosophy be said to have completed its task before reducing the dualism of intellect and being?"[19] Yes, it can and must, or else it will disintegrate into either a metaphysics of the subject or a metaphysics of the object. Kant, with remarkable fidelity to his own principles, refused to do this. Nevertheless, it can be done if the fundamental requirements of the critique are renounced, and realism is forced to transform either its principles or its conclusions, at the risk of never recovering either.

[19] Ibid., 427.

CHAPTER SIX

THE IMPOSSIBILITY OF CRITICAL REALISM

We have now examined several types of critical realism and in each instance have come to the conclusion that the critique of knowledge is essentially incompatible and irreconcilable with metaphysical realism. There is no middle ground. You must either begin as a realist with being, in which case you will have a knowledge of being, or begin as a critical idealist with knowledge, in which case you will never come in contact with being.

The method we have followed consists of presenting several concrete positions on a given problem and discussing their respective merits. Such an approach is necessary yet insufficient, for the fact that ten, twenty or a hundred philosophers have failed to find the solution to a problem does not prove that the problem is impossible to resolve. It should be noted, however, that the history of philosophy is not necessarily a dull empiricism. Those who think so are the victims of an illusion, the consequences of which have been felt only too often in this controversy. It is, of course, true that every philosophical doctrine carries with it a certain number of elements whose origin can be found in the time, place and circumstances in which it arose. These elements may be quantitatively far more important than the rest, and their study forms an integral part of the history of philosophy. On the other hand, every philosophical doctrine is ruled by the intrinsic necessity of its own position and by the consequences which flow from it in virtue of the universal law of reason. It often happens that the philosopher who originally defines one of these positions fails himself to see all the consequences which it entails. These consequences, however, are contained virtually within it, and it is always possible that another philosopher will discover them. The proper function of philosophical schools is precisely to uncover the consequences of principles, although those who formulated the principles may not have been aware of the consequences or, having perceived them, believed that they were not obliged to accept them. The dogmatic critique of philosophy may therefore be of considerable use if this critique is correctly conducted and the philosophy well chosen. When Regius, Descartes' disciple, deduced from the principles of his master that the existence of the external world is indemonstrable, he incurred the wrath of his master. He had seen, however, that the consequences flowed necessarily from the Cartesian method, and his conclusion was, from the first, accepted as valid by every idealist method.

What is true of Cartesianism is also true of the Kantian critique. It would be absurd to demand that those who claim to adopt a critical attitude should adhere to the letter of Kantianism. However, we do have the right to remind them of what the critique meant for Kant himself, and, when thus reminded, they are wrong to object that their adversaries are incapable of understanding any critique other than Kant's. If, as has happened, they add to this objection the accusation of historicism, the situation becomes particularly amusing, for they themselves are the most perfect example imaginable of historicism. To be valid, this accusation must suppose that the reason the critical version of the problem of knowledge has historically taken a certain form is because it was Kant's good pleasure to so conceive it, from which it naturally follows that each of us remains free to conceive it differently. In reality, the opposite is true. It was certainly not necessary for Kant to pose the critical problem; he could have, and perhaps should have, died without having done so. Once he did, however, Kant was duty bound to conform to the essence of this position, and he did. To recall the lesson of Kant to those who embrace the critique is therefore not to bind them to a man or a book, for even Kant's thought was obliged to yield to the formal necessities of the critical position once it had been conceived.

One of the most striking features of critico-realist literature is the lack of a definite meaning given to the word "critique". In fact, this word can signify practically any theory of knowledge in which dogmatic realism is not posited as self-evident. For example, we have seen that, if a philosophy wishes to indicate that its realism is not merely a bold affirmation based upon common sense alone, it calls itself critical. Critical realism, then, is opposed to naive realism. At other times the critical problem is defined as "the problem of the validity of human knowledge or, what amounts to the same thing, the ability of human thought to discover the truth". From this point of view, the refutation of radical skepticism and the correlative justification of dogmatism become a critical undertaking. Once dogmatism has been justified we may turn to this new problem: are we able to know an actual object distinct from knowledge itself, or do we only know knowledge? Once this new problem is solved the validity of realism, as opposed to idealism, will have been established critically. Supposing that we have established our ability to know something other than knowledge itself, it still remains to ask if we know the object as it is in itself or only, as phenomenalism would have it, as it appears to us. Critical realism will then have completed its task because it will have justified itself.[1]

That realism should then have refuted its adversaries, and even the adversaries of positions other than its own, we readily concede. It will thus have been shown to be critical toward others, and no one denies that it can and should be. But, if it be claimed that it is critical as regards itself, we must insist that that is a totally different question. There is no evidence that it ought to or even that it can be critical in this sense. However, if it does not adopt this last attitude, realism will not be critical as regards its own realism, and that is the whole question. If realism has the wherewithal to justify and conduct all the necessary critiques, it cannot itself be based upon any of them. A starting point for all of them, it is the product of none. In short, unlike critical idealism, which is critical to the extent that it is an idealism, any aspect of a realist philosophy may be subjected to criticism except its very realism. This is the true position of dogmatic realism which we defend.[2]

[1] Cf. C. Boyer, S.J., *Cursus Philosophiae* (Paris: Desclée de Brouwer, n.d.), 1:168–73.

[2] I must be excused for reminding those who would attribute some other position to me of my true position, although such a discussion will more likely than not be fruitless. Thus, Fr. Boyer (op. cit., 170, n. 1) attributes the following thesis to me: "Problema criticum ullo modo a scholasticis consideratum esse." Even supposing that I were speaking of scholastics in general, which was not the case, this thesis dug up by Fr. Boyer in no way affects my position. I have never denied that St. Thomas considered problems which Fr. Boyer discusses under the name "critical" nor that, in this sense, he posed the critical problem. I deny only that the problem, thus presented, deserves the name "critical", a thesis which Fr. Boyer does not even dream of discussing. The whole situation becomes even more comical when Fr. Descoqs reproaches me in his *Praelectiones theologiae naturalis* (1:48) for refusing to pose the critical problem because "it is self-contradictory": what is contradictory is critical realism or, more precisely still, the attempt to present the problem of critical idealism from the perspective of

Thus, there is nothing wrong with designating as critical the various refutations of skepticism, idealism or criticism, although from beginning to end they presuppose the validity of realism. Nevertheless, nothing that presupposes realism can serve to justify it critically. The rejection of the critique is not a critical position. Since it has never been successfully demonstrated that a critical realism can critically justify its very realism, it must be admitted that, if a precise meaning is required, the expression "critical realism" does not provide that meaning: it implies contradiction.

Once this first point has been established there are still several other issues to be clarified. First of all, each time we have discussed some particular form of critical realism and found it lacking, others have always claimed that another form of critical realism might overcome our objections. And if we then demonstrated the insufficiency of the next form of critical realism, still another was trotted out. The partisans of critical realism maintain that this process must continue until it has been proven that their position is impossible as a matter of principle. To this we reply that, if those who maintain that critical realism is possible in principle never provide a factual demonstration, it is a bit much for them to demand that their adversaries accept this doctrine on the strength of a promise of future proofs. It is up to them to show that it is indeed possible. The whole question would be resolved if they would only do that. While waiting, however, we may occupy our time profitably by demonstrating the inherent self-contradiction involved in each critical realism which has been advanced up to now and by inquiring whether this self-contradiction is not coessential with the very question asked.

Thomist realism. That is the extent of my thesis; it remains unscathed, for its opponents have been busy refuting something quite different.

A second defense commonly used by the critical realists consists of saying: as a matter of course, critical realism is impossible if the critique in question is understood in a Kantian sense, but Kant does not have the exclusive rights to the word "critique"; it is not impossible to conceive of a critique of knowledge different from his. Why, then, should we Aristotelian and Thomist realists not have a critique of our own?

Why, indeed, if not because those who claim to present the critical problem as realists do so only as a response to the Kantian statement of the problem. None of them cares to contest the obvious fact that they never would have dreamed of the critical problem if Kant had not done so. Most of them openly acknowledge that St. Thomas himself never thought of posing the critical problem, and they are thus free from the need to spend their time searching his writings for some formula that can be bent to their purposes. The fact is that for all these realists, the critical problem remains bound to its Kantian formulation, and, although some, like Fr. Maréchal, claim not to discuss the problem according to Kant's method, they seek to resolve the problem in opposition to Kant. It is their right to do so if it is possible, but there are conditions to the possibility of such an undertaking.

In order to resolve the problem and refute Kant it is necessary to pose the same problem he did, for resolving a problem can hardly consist of assuming that it is solved. If the problem is to be the same as Kant's, the formulation of the problem and the course of its discussion must circumscribe the same difficulty to which Kant claimed to have found the answer. Unless this fundamental condition is satisfied it will be incumbent upon critical realism to demonstrate that there is a critical problem of knowledge distinct both from Kant's and from the brute reaffirmation of dogmatic realism, the validity of which had been denied by Kant's critique. In other words, either you must do battle with Kant on his own ground by accepting his definition of the critical problem or you must discuss a quite distinct problem which simply uses the name "critique", and in that case Kant's critique will simply remain without a response.

As a matter of fact, the Aristotelian realisms which call themselves critical make quite certain not to state the question so rigorously. A certain amount of indeterminacy is necessary for their existence, and the reason they dislike being reminded of Kant is because the rigor of his example would make it difficult for them to maintain this state of indeterminacy. The disdain some of them show for history is explicable, at least in part, by the practical advantage they find in ignoring it. However, it is dangerous to ignore the history of philosophy, for, if you do, you are not ignoring contingent facts but necessary conceptual relationships.

Of course, we are not here concerned with absolute metaphysical necessities; if Kant's critique had been metaphysically necessary, it would have been true. However, it is possible to be aided in understanding the nature of an error by disengaging it from the historical contingencies which have given it the appearance of absolute necessity, the hypothetical and relative necessity which it possesses by virtue of its erroneous starting point. For critical philosophy was not born out of thin air. The idea developed slowly in the thought of a certain man living at a certain time and thinking in a philosophical setting that was historically determined. And since Kant himself, in the preface to the first edition of his *Critique of Pure Reason*, summarized for us the conditions in which critical philosophy was born, nothing could be more helpful to an understanding of his work than to examine with him those conditions.

In their simplest form these conditions can be reduced to the statement of an antinomy, itself inseparable from the structure of reason. There exists a certain type of knowledge, called metaphysical, in which reason is constrained to ask certain questions although it is unable to resolve them. The reason for this is that, in this undertaking, reason makes use of principles that are successfully applied to experience and are therefore valid. Since it sees that the details of experience are inexhaustible, however, reason is aware that it will never be able to complete the edifice of knowledge by these means. In order to do so it posits other principles which go beyond all experience, and from the moment the limits of experience are exceeded reason finds itself in the presence of conclusions which are, at the same time, necessary when considered in themselves but contradictory when compared to each other. This closed field given over to the interminable combat between theses which no experience can verify is called metaphysics.

The starting point of Kant's reflections is thus the empirical confirmation of a double fact: the incessant reoccurrence of metaphysical problems and the impossibility of their solution. These are the facts. Formerly the despotic queen of the sciences, metaphysics is now abandoned and despised by all. Locke had tried to justify it by a physiology of human understanding which sought to validate its pretensions to transcendent knowledge, but after a temporary revival dogmatism once again found itself checkmated. It was Hume who announced the fact, and his work merely marks the last step of a necessary evolution: a disgust for metaphysical knowledge, indifference and a skepticism which extended from metaphysics to science itself.

It was precisely at this point in time that some hope of changing this situation arose, for never had the natural sciences flourished as at the end of the eighteenth century, just when metaphysics appeared to be in its death throes.

Whatever arguments Hume may have advanced to show that no empirical knowledge can be necessary, Newton's physics was a living proof to the contrary. The resounding success of Newtonian physics and the enthusiasm with which it was greeted suggested to Kant a positive interpretation of the discredit into which metaphysics had fallen. Instead of regarding this discredit as the result of a senility of reason, he found in it proof that the faculty of judgment of an age matured by experience would no longer be content with the mere appearance of knowledge. Far from indicating a senility of reason, the general indifference of the eighteenth century with regard to metaphysics was a sign of maturity. The time had come for metaphysics to get acquainted with itself by setting up a tribunal that would guarantee its legitimate claims and exclude all others. The critique of pure reason was this tribunal. It would serve as the court of last resort, judging metaphysics in the name of the "eternal and immutable laws of reason".

Thus, Kant started from a historical experience. There was at least that much of empiricism at the outset of his undertaking. Of course this empirical starting point would be quickly left behind, since the critique would have as its object the discovery of the necessary reasons that science enjoys a success which metaphysics has been refused. It remains no less true that, as Kant himself said, it was only after all other avenues —dogmatism, psychological empiricism, skepticism—had been tried and tried in vain that he embarked upon the critique, "the only road left open". What the *Prolegomena* says about the effect produced upon Kant by his reading of Hume entirely confirms the testimony of the first preface to the *Critique*. Hume's critique had been for Kant the death blow to metaphysics. After that there was nothing left to do but search for the cause of its death in the very nature of reason.

Such an undertaking, a judgment of the validity of metaphysics' claims, thus presupposes a certain conception of metaphysics itself. More precisely, it presupposes that metaphysics be conceived, after the manner of Descartes, Leibniz and Wolf, as an abstract rationalism devoid of all empirical content, owing its preeminent position to its perfect isolation from sensible knowledge. When Kant declares that the origin of all metaphysics' troubles is reason's claim to a knowledge attained "independently of all experience", it is clear that he has forgotten the existence of a metaphysics like that of Aristotle or St. Thomas Aquinas. His formula, which applies in full to Descartes and Leibniz, leaves classical metaphysics untouched. I know quite well what objections Kant would have raised, but it is a fact that he did not take classical metaphysics into consideration. The immediate consequence of this oversight was that, instead of criticizing metaphysics, Kant criticized its two bastard offspring which the eighteenth century had bequeathed him: on the one hand a rigorous but empty rationalism, on the other hand a concrete empiricism devoid of all necessity. Having lost the notion of a rational knowledge fertilized by an intelligible datum, he had no other recourse but to deduce the intelligibility of experience from knowledge. Thus Kant was able to obtain an experiential knowledge that was both concrete and necessary, but by locating the unique source of the intelligibility of experience in knowledge he confined it within the limits of its own perfection and shut it off from any external contribution capable of fertilizing it.

This is why Kant could not avoid accepting the empty formalism of the very metaphysics he had criticized. He had no deep knowledge of any empiricism other than Hume's invertebrate psychologism, and, considering with reason that this was a sure source of skepticism, he could not help but prefer an unempirical rationalism to an irrational empiricism. If, therefore, his critique sought a knowledge that would be proof against all skepticism, he would have to be content with a knowledge that was independent of experience, like that of Cartesian metaphysics, on the chance of limiting its bearing upon reason to its experiential independence. Such knowledge is what Kant called pure knowledge. Applied to knowledge (and later to morality), the epithet "pure" always signifies, for Kant, "pure from any empirical element". As he says himself: "All knowledge is pure which is free from any external element. But knowledge is absolutely pure when it is free from all experience of sensation." If this is so, pure knowledge has no *a posteriori* element; knowledge will therefore be absolutely pure when it is completely *a priori*.

Starting with these givens, the notion of "pure reason" itself becomes intelligible. There is pure reason if there is pure knowledge, that is, entirely *a priori* knowledge. Now, when the problem is presented in these terms another problem arises. To find *a priori* judgments is not difficult. All analytical judgments are *a priori* since they are judgments in which the relation of predicate to subject is one of identity, but although these judgments are evident they are also sterile. When I say: bodies are extended, I formulate an obvious analytical judgment, for the notion of extension is included in the notion of a body; but I merely explain my knowledge, I do not extend it. Now, science is only constructed by the acquisition and enrichment of knowledge; therefore, we must seek its origin in synthetic judgments.

Synthetic judgments are those judgments in which the predicate is not identical with the subject. As with analytic judgments, it is easy to give an example of a synthetic judgment, for all empirical judgments are of this type. But we have just said, and with reason, that the knowledge we are looking for must be *a priori*, since necessity cannot be derived from experience. What we need, therefore, are judgments that are both synthetic and *a priori*. Now, in all the sciences, necessary judgments are of this type. For example, in mathematics, a *straight* line (quality) is the *shortest* route (quantity) between two points. Likewise, in physics, the *quantity* of matter is unaffected by *change*; in any *communication* of movement, action and reaction must be equal. These judgments are both synthetic and *a priori*. If we were to suppose that metaphysics is a science, even in a rough form, it also would have to contain judgments of this sort. Hume claimed that there are no such judgments in metaphysics; if this is true, metaphysics is not a science. It is true that Hume also denied the existence of such judgments in physics and mathematics, but if Hume had been right about that, neither physics nor metaphysics would exist as sciences. Now, these sciences do exist; therefore, the judgments which make these sciences possible must also exist. In order to determine the general conditions of scientific knowledge it will therefore be necessary and sufficient to answer three questions. How is pure mathematics possible? How is pure physics possible? How is pure metaphysics possible, at least insofar as it represents a natural disposition and need of reason? To search throughout each branch of knowledge for whatever synthetic *a priori* knowledge it contains is to search for what constitutes each one as a science. Thus, the claim of each branch of knowledge to the title "science" must be justified. This cannot be done without judging, which is to say without criticizing, the merit of each claim. Therefore, the critique of reason consists of seeking the synthetic *a priori* principles of mathematics, physics and metaphysics and of determining what they are and what conditions these disciplines must satisfy to function as sciences.

Thus conceived, the critique of knowledge is presented to us with definite characteristics which fix its place among the other branches of philosophy. First of all, it is a *distinct* science: "a particular science which can be called critique of pure reason". Furthermore, since it deals only with the conditions of our synthetic *a priori* judgments concerning certain classes of objects, it is constituted on a plane which is prior to that of our experience of these objects. This must necessarily be so, since it studies the conditions which make experience possible. The critique is therefore a *transcendental* knowledge with regard to experience. Finally, since it deals with those conditions of experience which are within reason itself, it is a critique of *pure* reason: free from all empirical elements. Thus, the Kantian critique is a conscious, fully defined undertaking, for it is its transcendental *a priori* character that makes it a critique. We must either accept the content of knowledge as it is presented to us, as empirically given fact, in which case it will be impossible to judge it, or we must seek to judge it, in which case we will need to place ourselves outside of knowledge in order to attain a point of view from which such a judgment is possible. The only conceivable point of view of this sort is that of their conditions in the thinking subject. Thus, the very possibility of the critique as a science is strictly bound to the transcendental attitude, which consists of seeking the *a priori* conditions of the possibility of objects within pure reason.

Whether or not we accept Kant's position, there can be no doubt that the critique is, in his thought, an undertaking which is defined by its method as well as by its goal. Let us suppose for the present that a realism claims for itself the title "critical"; what distinct meaning can we give to this term?

It could not be the meaning Kant intended. A realism which is justified from the point of view of the pure *a priori* conditions of experience, to the radical exclusion of any empirical given whatsoever, cannot help but arrive at Kantian conclusions. It will end up in a Kantian world of experience in which objects receive their intelligibility from *a priori* conditions which constitute them as objects. Even supposing that we wish to call this Kantian world of experience realist, this "subjective realism" will not come to the defense of classical metaphysics. An objective realism of the Aristotelian type cannot be justified by Kant's critique, understood as Kant himself understood it.

It might be possible to start from within the critical position in order somehow to force the knowing subject to go beyond itself and make contact with things in themselves. But here we would come in conflict not merely with the letter of the Kantian critique but with the spirit from which it was born. Kant's critique is not content simply to ignore the question of what things-in-themselves are; it actually forbids any such question. It is of the very essence of the critical spirit to pose all questions from the point of view of the *a priori* conditions of knowledge and strictly to forbid all other questions. For example, the study of the conditions of knowledge must be related to two sources: sensibility and understanding. It is therefore necessary to posit both. If we ask if these two conditions of experience arise from a common source, Kant will respond: perhaps, but this source is unknown to us; there is therefore no point in spending any time trying to discover it.

Fichte was only able to escape Kant's veto by becoming involved in dogmatic metaphysics, that is, by renouncing the critical spirit. The same principles are involved in the problem with which we are here concerned. To accept the critique with the intention of going beyond it is not to accept it at all, for it is of the essence of the critique to forbid all attempts to go beyond it. It issues an *a priori* prohibition against any speculation beyond its narrow confines. We freely admit that the practitioner of the critique is well aware that his world of experience is a facade and that beyond the facade there is something else, but he is unable to look at the other side of the facade in order to see what is there because, each time he tries, the *a priori* conditions of experience change into a new facade hiding behind the old one. This constant substitution of new facades for old ones is scientific progress, but the critique implies by definition that if the facade is always able to retreat before us, we will never be able to get past it. This is why there is no more hopeless undertaking than to try to change a critical idealist's mind by first accepting his statement of the problem, for his statement of the problem forbids the asking of any other questions, and the critique implies the negation of what is needed to get us beyond it.

When you reach the most basic level of their texts, it is difficult not to wonder if some neo-scholastics are not more concerned with convincing themselves than with converting idealists. When a neo-scholastic does little more than devise means of appearing to pose the critical problem it is because he himself is not sure whether or not he too should pose the critical problem. Many of them seem to lack confidence in their own position. After Descartes, whose principles were the conscious negation of their principles, had been obliged to prove that the external world exists, they wondered how their own philosophy, which was wholly based upon knowledge of the external world, could formulate a like proof. After Kant, whose doctrine was the radical negation of their dogmatic metaphysics, required the critique as a prolegomenon to every metaphysics, they asked themselves how their own dogmatism could be justified by the critique. It would seem that, for them, the history of philosophy is an undifferentiated whole, so that whenever one philosophy asks a question, all other philosophies must ask the very same question. This is why we see so many Thomists and Aristotelians seeking to obtain from Aristotle and St. Thomas answers to problems which were brought about by the abandonment of classical realism. They are engaged in what could be called a "naive criticism", one in which it is sufficient proof that there actually is a critical problem to say: someone has posed it.[3]

The good faith of those who think this way is so ironclad that some of them do not hesitate to accuse those who take exception of bad faith. But there are many signs which should be enough to warn them that they have reached a dead end. First of all, as we have noted several times, almost all of these so-called critiques of knowledge begin by accepting a metaempirical grasp of the absolute self, which may not be necessary for realism but which eliminates in advance any critical statement of the question. Then, having established at the outset the absolute knowledge of the self,[4] they undertake to prove the existence of the external world in the name of what they call a critique of knowledge. In reality, no critique of knowledge is able, much less required, to advance such a proof, for this is not a problem raised by the critique. Kant himself professes an immediate realism of the experience of external objects, given as such, in the *a priori* form of space; in other words, he affirms an immediate

---

[3] There are a variety of expressions revealing a similar spirit in G. Picard, *Le Problème critique fondamental*, 78; L. Noël, *Notes d'épistémologie thomiste*, 23; Roland-Gosselin, *Essai d'une étude critique de la connaissance* 11; P. Descoqs, *Praelectiones theologiae naturalis*, 1:55–56; C. Boyer, *Cursus philosophiae*, 1:205.

[4] For example, G. Picard, op. cit., 57. P. Descoqs, *Praelectiones*, 50.

realism of the existence of a Kantian external world. As for the existence of another world, that of things-in-themselves which cause phenomena, he simply takes it for granted as Fichte and L. Brunschvicq will do after him. There is no question of neglect here, nor has the critique simply glossed over a problem, for the refusal to consider the question is bound to the very essence of the critique. The trancendental point of view of the *a priori* conditions of the object of knowledge ignores, by definition, the empirical problem of the existence in themselves of known objects. The result is that, by a paradox which should even surprise them, "critical realists" are today absolutely the only ones who pose the problem of the existence of the external world, and they do so in the name of exigencies of a critique which itself professes to ignore the problem.[5]

[5] Thus, for example, Fr. Descoqs maintains without hesitation that a realist critique of being is possible (see, on this subject, his *Praelectiones,* 1:41). The adversary he set up against himself would say: Being? Either I affirm it, and then there can be no critique, or I deny it, in which case it is impossible, by definition, to affirm it. According to Fr. Descoqs, there is a third approach which is equally possible: "Since it is a given that there is being (object) in the face of which it is impossible not to think (subject), we must ask what the value of being is, and, therefore, what the value of truth is, which is to say, the relation between subject and object" (41). Concerning the above, we must observe that these formulas, so precise at first glance, are actually ambiguous. Taken at face value, they present the critical problem, or at least they can be understood in such a sense. If by "being", object is understood, and if by "object", immanent object is understood, we are faced with the critical problem.

If, on the contrary, we understand "object" to mean object in itself, the critical problem is negated in advance. Finally, if the question is left open and no prior judgments are made concerning the reality of the object, we must then admit that it is not evident that the being spontaneously affirmed by thought is the being of an object in itself. It then becomes necessary to prove (or deny) its existence; we therefore end up

From this, in all the doctrines we have examined except Fr. Maréchal's,[6] flows a complete confusion between the

_____

proceeding from thought to being. This is why Fr. Descoqs rallies to the aid of Fr. Picard (38) in defending the possibility of giving the *cogito* a legitimate meaning (40), and the logical and psychological necessity of considering the cognitive order before the ontological order (*A nosse ad esse,* 43; this is therefore a variety of hybrid idealist realism); he also supports the necessity of doubting as a universal method (48). What seems to have led Fr. Descoqs into this error is the difficulty he has in understanding why his adversaries refuse to pose the problem. He believes it is because, in their eyes, the critical problem "is self-contradictory" (48). By no means: what is contradictory is the attempt to pose the problem from the perspective of classical realism. You can raise the critical problem without any contradiction, but you cannot join it to the conclusions of St. Thomas. The citation from Kant (45, n.) illustrates the difficulty; Kant's critique bases a dogmatism upon the reduction of metaphysics to the status of a science (like physics) while rendering it entirely *a priori*, that is, by ruining the realism Fr. Descoqs wants to establish.

⁶ It is fitting to add to Fr. Maréchal's attempt Fr. G. Rabeau's recent effort, *Le Jugement d'existence* (Paris: J. Vrin, 1938). It is the work of a true philosopher whose deepest convictions tend toward realism but who hopes to arrive there by means of a method analogous to L. Brunschvicg's in *La Modalité du jugement.* All the difficulties inherent in attempts of this sort arise in this remarkable and profound work. First, we must remember that realism is disavowed in advance by the criticism of *La Modalité du jugement.* In every criticism conscious of its essence, and none is more so than L. Brunschvicg's, existence is not a predicate; there is, therefore, no conceivable way of arriving at an actual existence at the end of a judgment. In short, Fr. Rabeau expects a critical method to solve his problem, while it is of the essence of the critique not to raise it. Inversely, since he raised this problem in terms of the critical method, Fr. Rabeau is led to search the works of St. Thomas for some sign that the apprehension of actual existence is the work of an intellect in its function of judging. From this, in another work by the same author (*Species Verbum: L'Activité intellectuelle élémentaire selon saint Thomas d'Aquin* [Paris: J. Vrin, 1938]), flow a whole series of investigations designed to

point of view of the critique and of Cartesian idealism.[7] Overcome with zeal for critical idealism just when it is finally dying, these realists feel called upon to search in what Descartes directed against them in 1641 for weapons against what Kant directed against Descartes and themselves in 1781. It seems to them that they would be critical philosophers if they were able to make do with an aborted realism, which Malebranche and Berkeley had long ago shown to be bankrupt and which Kant's criticism had no less radically eliminated than had Aristotle's. In fact, their pretensions are reduced to still less, for they claim to demand of Descartes that he dispense them from posing his problem as well as Kant's. The *cogito* they invoke puts them in possession of an absolute principle,[8] that is, a principle valid for all

---

discover in St. Thomas a *"species intelligibilis of actual existence"* (148), as if it were the intellect alone rather than the whole man which apprehends existence in the doctrine of St. Thomas. Everyone must admire the philosophical profundity of pp. 156–58 and 186–87. All the talent and effort put into the attempt to find an exit from this dead end failed, but they at least proved this much: this is indeed a dead end. The efforts of a true philosopher are never wasted.

[7] This confusion is evident in R. Jolivet's work, *Le Thomisme et la critique de la connaissance,* in which the author asks himself (20) if the critical problem must necessarily be presented in Cartesian terms. Most assuredly not: Descartes is historically at the origin of critical idealism, but he himself never conceived of it, and if you pose the problem of knowledge in Cartesian terms, you will wind up in a dogmatic idealism rather than a critical realism.

[8] It is in this way that R. Jolivet seeks a solution to the "critical" problem: in a non-Cartesian *cogito.* Now, while it is true that the *cogito* (a statement of fact that I am, since I think) is not in itself bound to idealism, it becomes fatally linked to idealism when an appeal is made to it in order to pose and resolve the problem of knowledge. If you begin with a *cogito* which "does not imply idealism" (21) and which also considers that "the problem of existence is an arbitrary problem that cannot

being insofar as it is. This is as much as to say that in the light of this immediate evidence the critical problem need never have been posed. But once we are introduced by the *cogito* into realist metaphysics, we will be able to do without both Descartes and Kant, since the aptitude of thought for grasping a being, insofar as it is what it is, guarantees this aptitude in regard to all being. Therefore, it will be necessary to pretend to solve Kant's problem by pretending to solve Descartes' and, in order to do this, we will have incorrectly stated the only problem we really wished to solve: why do we say that the external world exists?

---

be imposed upon us and which we must absolutely refuse" (20–21), then you will be faced neither with the idealist problem nor the critical problem. In fact, although your starting point may well carry the name of the *cogito*, it may just as well use a different name, for there is no reason to use the name *cogito* for the starting point of a philosophy unless the fact that I think is the starting point. It is useless to claim that St. Augustine did so (19–20), for no one denies that the *cogito* has a place in realism; the whole question is whether it can serve as its foundation. Now, St. Augustine's *cogito* is a weapon, and a very effective one, against absolute skepticism, but it is certainly not the starting point for a justification of realism. Nor is it any more so for R. Jolivet, for whom "realism is not demonstrated" (27). If a realism which is not demonstrated claims to be critical, there is nothing more to be said. The word "critical" is thus emptied of all distinctive meaning. This is what R. Jolivet does, while maintaining against all evidence that, for Kant, the critical problem consisted of posing a problem which is "a medieval problem" (34). The critical problem consists, "for Kant", of constructing "the science of the limitations of human reason" from the point of view of the pure, *a priori* conditions of knowledge. The fact that Kant admits the existence of external beings does not authorize Jolivet to say that "the Kantian position is no different from the medieval position" (34), unless the medieval exteriority of beings in regard to the knowing subject is confused with the Kantian exteriority of things-in-themselves in regard to knowledge. These are two totally different problems.

Thus, the expression "critical realism" has been understood in many senses, but these senses are legitimate only when the expression which designates them is not "critical realism". The expression may mean that realism is not reduced to positing itself as a reflex affirmation based only upon what is called common sense. Critical realism is then opposed to naive realism, and nothing could be more legitimate than such an attitude, for it is true that realism must go far beyond common sense to attain a true foundation; but in that case it is more correctly named philosophical realism. Critical realism may also mean that realism must somehow defend itself against idealism and is capable of criticizing the critique itself, even of accusing it of a failure to be truly critical. This is also true, but every critique directed by realism against its adversaries presupposes the validity of realism; it is then a question of realism judging idealism, and here the critique is totally subordinate to realism. Finally, every realism that defines truth as the conformity of the intellect with what is may be called "critical", striving to distinguish between knowledge which truly conforms to what is and knowledge which does not. Such a realism is necessarily engaged in criteriology and as a consequence also in the theory of knowledge, and it is impossible to do this without criticizing and judging. Nothing is more necessary, but here again this critique will only be realist because it presupposes a realist notion of truth. It is necessary to choose between Aristotle and St. Thomas (truth is the conformity of intelligence with what is) and Kant in his logic (truth is the accord of reason with itself). Shall we judge reality as a function of knowledge or knowledge as a function of reality? That is the whole question. Since we are dealing with a realism that criticizes, it is necessary for realism to be posited before the critique which it establishes and to which it cannot be subordinate.

We can say, therefore, that a realist theory of knowledge and a realist critique of knowledge are both possible and necessary, but neither the one nor the other is equivalent to critical realism, and they should not be called by that name. On the other hand, when you engage in a critique *veri nominis*, it goes without saying that the resulting doctrine has the right to claim an origin in the critique, but it loses the right to call itself realist because, in the existential judgment to which we are led, existence itself is no more than a postulate or a predicate. The fact that some have resigned themselves to this fate proves the degree to which three centuries of idealism have obliterated in us the profound sense of existential realism upon which all classical philosophy was based. We must therefore seek to recover the meaning of the verb "to be".

CHAPTER SEVEN

THE KNOWING SUBJECT

The methods of the various realisms we have discussed all agree in approaching the problem of existence from the standpoint of knowledge, and in the process the knowing subject is reduced to just that: knowledge. From this arises a whole series of problems which must remain insoluble for those philosophers who wish to remain realists in the tradition of Aristotle and St. Thomas Aquinas.

To which faculty of knowledge shall a Thomist attribute the apprehension of existence? The first faculty to come to mind might be sensibility. But a sensation is the apprehension of a sensible quality which affects a sense organ, such as color, odor, taste, etc. Now, since existence is not a sensible quality we have no sense organ with which to perceive it. Therefore, existence is not apprehended by any one sense. Moreover, since existence is not a sensible quality it cannot be one of those common sensibles, like movement, which are perceived by several different senses. Therefore, we do not grasp existence by means of the senses.

The term "existence" designates a concept. Therefore, it might seem that we should seek its origin in the intellect. But here again there are serious difficulties. Suppose that we start from the fact that everything we know is presented to us as within the order of being and that it is impossible for us to think except in terms of being. The fact is unquestionable, but a necessity of thought does not guarantee the existence of a concrete, extramental reality. To prove that it does in a special instance, the ego, does not prove that the extrapolation of this evidence to all other cases is anything but a sophism or an unjustifiable psychological illusion.

We might add that the intellect does more than merely *think* in terms of being: it apprehends being. This also is true, but the being the intellect apprehends is being in general. Even when we conceive of it as attributable to a particular subject the intellect does not conceive the existential actuality of this particular being; we simply drape our concept of being-in-general over the subject, like a blanket that will serve to designate every existence but not a particular one. In short, while only individuals exist, the intellect is able to conceive only what is general. Therefore, existence as such escapes the grasp of the intellect.

We thus find ourselves confronted with a dilemma the terms of which St. Thomas has clearly defined: "Est enim sensus particularium, intellectus vero universalium."[1] It matters little that existence is singular; since it is not a sensible quality the senses cannot perceive it. Nor does it matter that existence is intelligible, since it is not intelligible to us in its singularity. It would seem, therefore, that existence is unknowable to us.

Note, however, that the difficulties encountered in this regard are caused by the manner in which the problem is presented. To demand that sense or intellect alone should grasp existence is to demand the impossible. Moreover, since neither sense nor intellect alone is able to grasp existence, no abstract combination of the two will yield what neither can do of itself. The problem can never be resolved from the standpoint of knowledge in general; rather, it

[1] St. Thomas Aquinas, *In II de Anima,* lect. 5 (Pirotta ed.), n. 284.

must be resolved in terms of the knowing subject. At least this is the only way to resolve the problem while remaining faithful to the spirit of classical realism, which is simply the natural realism of human reason. As St. Thomas says: "Non enim proprie loquendo sensus aut intellectus cognoscit, sed homo per utrumque."[2] This explains why we are able to form a certain knowledge of singulars. By means of the senses we directly grasp the things we know, thanks to our perception of their sensible qualities; and by means of the intellect we grasp the same things, thanks to the abstract concepts we form of them. Therefore, it is the whole man who knows particular things, in that he thinks what he perceives.

However, this is not the precise problem whose resolution we are seeking. Although the two questions are closely connected, explaining man's knowledge of particulars is not the same as explaining man's knowledge of the existence of particulars. The two questions remain distinct even though it is true that the particular alone exists, for we are concerned with discovering how existence is known by the knowing human subject. Much has already been done to define the point of view from which we may hope to find an answer to this question. Several interpreters of classical realism have done so with exquisite exactitude, and at least one of them has had the wisdom to hold fast to it. "Actually, it is by means of a sort of metaphor", says Domet de Vorges, "that we say that the senses know this or the intellect knows that. Properly speaking, neither the senses nor the intellect knows; it is the individual man who knows by means of the senses and the intellect. There are several actions but only one subject, one being who possesses distinct yet harmonious powers and produces these diverse actions."

---

[2] St. Thomas Aquinas, *Quaest. disp. de Veritate*, q. 2, a. 6, ad 3.

Others after him have reached the same conclusion,[3] one which St. Thomas, in his polemic against the Averroist doctrine of the separate intellect, indicated was the only acceptable conclusion. Aristotle had already said in his *De Anima*, I, 4, 408b, 13–15: "It is better to say, not that the soul suffers, learns or reasons, but that man does through the soul." Concerning such operations St. Thomas comments: "Non sunt animae tantum, sed conjuncti." This also explains his relentless opposition to the Averroist separation of the intellect: "*Homo* autem est perfectissimus inter omnia inferiora moventia. Ejus autem propria et naturalis operatio est intelligere." To locate the principle of his proper activity beyond or above him is simply to say that man is not man.[4] No question can be validly approached from the standpoint of sense or intellect alone; everything must, in the long run, be related to the *conjunctum*, to man, who is the only concretely existing knowing subject.

This viewpoint is no longer familiar to our contemporaries, even when all their natural tendencies incline them toward realism. For starting with the *conjunctum* means starting with corporeal bodies as well as with knowledge, and if we start

---

[3] Domet de Vorges, *La perception et la psychologie thomiste*, (Paris: Roger and Chernoviz, 1892), 197. All of chap. 12, "De la perception totale de l'être individuel", is oriented in the proper direction and even today remains very useful. You will find at least the principle of the solution correctly formulated by C. Sentroul, *Kant et Aristote*, 2nd ed. (Paris: F. Alcan, 1913), 306; and N. B. Zamboni, "La Gnoseologia dell'atto, come fondamento della filosofia dell'essere", *Vita e Pensiero* (Milan, n.d.), 84. These two authors, especially the second, have meditated profoundly on the problem and have followed their own personal ways in attempting a solution. Whether he wanted to or not, Msgr. Zamboni returned, 87–89, to Maine de Biran.

[4] St. Thomas Aquinas, *Summa Cont. Gent.* II, 76, at "Item, in natura cujuslibet moventis . . ." and the following paragraph.

with bodies it is clear that, for us, the existence of matter is not a problem. Now, for centuries others have considered the existence of matter to be problematic. How, then can we speak as if the problem did not exist without excluding ourselves from philosophical discourse? This inquiry cannot be simply terminated after a realist has recalled and proclaimed the primary truth that the whole man is the true knowing subject. Once we have agreed that the natural starting point for a realist noetic is the knowing subject, we must still come to some agreement concerning the nature of the subject. Even then the prestige of idealism may trouble the philosopher's spirit and cause him to lose the ground he had gained. Thus, for example, Fr. Joseph Gredt starts out correctly by upholding the validity of natural realism against critical realism. With reason, he notes that every critical realism is either an empty title or implies an illationism analogous to Descartes', Malebranche's and that demonstrated by some modern scholastics. "Natural realism", says Fr. Gredt, "is opposed to critical realism, and it is through natural realism that we have an immediate knowledge of transsubjective objects, both in sense knowledge and intellectual knowledge. Our thesis upholds natural realism."[5] At first glance it would be impossible to ask for more precise statements, but upon closer examination difficulties begin to crop up.

What are we to understand by "transsubjective objects"? The answer to this question depends upon the meaning of the word "subject". In Fr. Gredt's doctrine "transsubjective objects are those objects which are distinguishable from knowledge not only objectively but also subjectively in the order of being." This definition obviously assumes that the

[5] J. Gredt, O.S.B., *Elementa philosophiae aristotelico-thomisticae,* 5th ed. (Freiburg im Breisgau: Herder, 1920), 2:69–70.

subject in question is knowledge, from which it follows that whatever really exists outside of knowledge is transsubjective in the fullest sense. Thus, the body of a knowing subject is transsubjective with regard to that very subject. To put it another way, for an object to be transsubjective it is not necessary that the object be distinct from the body of the knowing subject and its affections. From this point of view the sound received in the basilar membrane and the warmth and pressure felt by the sensing subject are physical, transsubjective objects. "Haec non sunt quidem transsomatica, at sunt transpsychica, transsubjectiva."[6]

Fr. Gredt's natural realism thus presupposes that the body of the knowing subject is not itself a part of the knowing subject but subsists in itself, outside the subject, with all the sensible affections whose focal point it is. Such a hypothesis introduces a profound modification into Thomist realism, or rather, it burdens realism with problems which a natural realism would never have posed for itself. Properly speaking, the only knowing subject a natural realism may start with is man. It is aware of no other for the simple reason that there is no other. To imagine, as Fr. Gredt does, a knowing subject in addition to which there is a transsubjective body, itself surrounded by transsomatic subjects, is to consider the distinction between body and soul as philosophically equivalent to the distinction between our bodies and other bodies. Nothing could be more foreign to such a doctrine than the fundamental positions of classical realism in which the knowing subject is, and can only be, the substance Man, the union of soul and body.

Because he forgot this, Fr. Gredt became involved in a type of mediatism that was contrary to his deepest intentions.

---

[6] Ibid., 68.

The external senses are manifestly inseparable from the body. Therefore, inasmuch as they are corporeal, they are relegated to the order of the transsubjective and are distinct from the knowing subject. To use Fr. Gredt's own terminology, we would say that the immediate object of the external senses, while not the transsomatic, is nevertheless the transpsychic and therefore also the transsubjective.[7] From this it follows that two mediations are necessary. The first is between sensible, somatic beings and their transsomatic objects; this first mediation will be the work of the senses.[8] The other mediation is between these somatic, transsubjective beings and the knowing subject. Is this second mediation possible? Supposing that it is, how shall it be carried out? Nobody will tell us, and for lack of this indispensable foundation the entire superstructure of this realism is in danger of collapsing.

This indifference with regard to such an important problem would be inexplicable, except that this doctrine ultimately resigns itself to becoming two realisms subsisting side by side without telling us how the two may be reconciled. Fr. Gredt did in fact maintain, with no qualifications, the validity of natural realism, according to which the external senses know their object immediately as transsubjective. Yet it is equally true that, for Fr. Gredt, the immediately given transsubjectivity is limited to what is sensibly given, so that the transsubjectivity of the object is linked to the transsubjectivity of the body, which is posited as external to the knowing subject. This natural or physical realism is thus a realism of the purely sensible. Conversely, the realism of the intellect, which is the realism of the incorporeal knowing subject, is not a physical but a metaphysical realism

[7] Ibid., 74, n. 689, Scholia.
[8] Ibid., 76, 2.

which only comes to grips with being as it is conceived abstractly, rather than grasping concrete acts of existence. In this doctrine the being which is grasped by intellectual knowledge is offered to us as a transsubjective reality, in the sense that its content is imposed upon the intellect with an objective necessity. The material content, so to speak, of an abstract intellectual truth does not depend upon the intellect; rather, the intellect depends upon it. Yet this objective existence itself is a product of the intellect,[9] so that, all told, the realism of the intellect is a metaphysical realism of the possible: "Mundus physicus obicitur sensibus secundum esse suum physicum, mundus metaphysicus obicitur cognitioni abstractae intellectus secundum realitatem suam metaphysicam (secundum esse suum possibile)."[10]

This separation of realism into a physical realism of the real and a metaphysical realism of the possible corresponds exactly to the separation of the knowing subject into a transsubjective subject and the properly subjective subject. It goes without saying that in such a doctrine intellectual knowledge as such necessarily remains confined within a subject to which being, in its physical actuality, can have no access. Therefore, this is still only a partial realism. Now, if it is true that every partial idealism is, in part, a realism, it is also true that every partial realism is, in part, an idealism. In order to recover a pure realism it is obviously necessary to join physical and metaphysical realism within the substantial unity of man. In short, in place of Fr. Gredt's knowing subject, it is necessary to substitute the *conjunctum*, the only true knowing subject.

To make this radical decision is also to accept the existence of the human body. It is therefore necessary to turn

[9] Ibid., 70-71, n. 687.
[10] Ibid., 77, n. 690, 2.

our attention to the classic objection against every position of this sort, namely, that to refuse to justify the existence of the external world by means of the critical reflection is simply to set up a postulate.

What, then, is a postulate? It is a proposition which must be accepted as true, although it is neither evident nor demonstrable. Any manual on the logic of the sciences will present this definition. If the proposition in question is evident, it is an axiom or principle, not a postulate. If the proposition is demonstrable, it is neither a postulate nor a principle but a conclusion. Thus, the postulate named after Euclid is an assumption which is presented as such. It is impossible to justify it by means of a demonstration, yet it is equally impossible to deny it without contradiction. Therefore, if someone asks if the existence of the external world is a postulate, the first response must be to ask in turn: to whom is the question presented?

If the question is addressed to an intellectualist philosophy, the existence of the external world is certainly a mere postulate. For pure, abstract thought, the existence of the corporeal world is neither evident nor demonstrable. The proof of this is that from this point of view it is always possible to deny the external world without self-contradiction. Berkeley's metaphysics is of such a type, perfectly consistent, so that once the starting point is granted you can run through it from one end to the other without falling into the least sophism or contradiction. This explains the initial impression of profundity which Berkeley makes upon the neophyte philosopher. His philosophy seems at once unbelievable yet irrefutable. It is, in fact, irrefutable on its home ground. It is futile to attempt to discover a flaw in its argument. It is the metaphysics of a possible world which God could have created if he had so desired, rather than creating our world, and in such a possible world Berkeley's philosophy would be not only consistent but true. But his is not a true metaphysics because it is not a science of the first principles and causes of the world in which we live.

Suppose, however, that the question were put to a metaphysical realist. He would respond without a doubt that the existence of the external world is, for man, self-evident and not a postulate at all. Of course, the idealist is free to maintain that this is really a postulate fallaciously disguised as self-evident, but the idealist may only do so because he himself refuses to give credence to sensible experience, which alone can raise this assertion above the status of a postulate. The fact that it is a postulate for the idealist does not at all mean that it must be one for the realist. As for the objection that if the existence of the external world is evident for one person it must be so for all, this is a very serious objection but by no means a decisive one. The real question is to ascertain whether the existence of the external world is self-evident to all men, including the idealist philosopher, insofar as they are human. After all, why should idealists refuse to think, as philosophers, the way they think as men? That is another question. For the moment, the question occupying our attention is not to know whether the existence of the external world is or is not philosophically evident but to know whether it is evident. To know this, we must describe the certainty we have that the external world exists and assign it a place amidst our thoughts.

If we turn to the testimony of experience, which we should do at the beginning of any undertaking, it would seem difficult to designate by any other word than "evident" the type of certitude we have concerning the existence of the external world. The actual existence of the page I am writing or the one you are reading is not an intellectual evidence of the axiomatic type, for it is possible for this page to be elsewhere, nor would it be self-contradictory for this page to have never been written. On the other hand, I need not ask that it be accepted as a postulate, for sensible perception is normally accompanied by an immediate certitude so clear that we hardly care to question it. No one really doubts that sight, touch, hearing, taste and even smell are normally competent to attest to existence, and whenever it is necessary to verify the existence of anything it is to the testimony of one or more of the senses that we turn.

This conviction of the reliability of our senses is simply the self-evidence of our experience. Since we are here concerned with self-evidence, it is futile to demand a demonstration. All we can do for one who does not see something is point it out to him. If he then sees it, well and good, but we cannot prove to him that he does see it. The difficulties begin only when the philosopher undertakes to transform this sensible certitude into a demonstrative certitude of the intellect. Here is the source of the classical idealist objections against the testimony of the senses. Illusions, dreams, hallucinations, the whole gamut of pathological states so dear to skeptics and idealists of all sorts are now brought forward. The idealist philosophers seem to believe their own arguments, but there is not a one without a flaw in it. The use they make of them in epistemology presupposes the acceptance of a well-known type of sophism: the shift from one genus to another. In effect, they demand that empirical fact should fulfill the requirements of the logic of abstract concepts. The argument boils down to saying: there are false perceptions which are taken to be true; therefore, it can never be known with certainty whether a perception is true or false. To hear those who reason in this manner, you would think that an abstract, ideal class of perceptions exists in which all perceptions find a place, even false ones. Having thus fabricated a class of "what has the appearance of a perception", you now declare that you are unable to distinguish between true and false perceptions and then conclude that this can never be done. This is as much as to say that, because there are colorblind persons affected by acholoropsy, no one can ever be sure that what he sees is not green.

Why do they adopt this posture? Because, having treated the sensible order in the same way as the conceptual, as decreed by idealism, those who reason in this manner require abstract demonstrations of sensible experience. It goes without saying that this is impossible, not because sensible experience lacks self-evidence, but because it is doubly sophistical to try to demonstrate what is self-evident and to do so following premises that arise in a different order of knowledge. Dreams, illusions, deliriums and hallucinations are neither essences nor distinct substances from which it would be possible to deduce conclusions valid for a genus or species. They are empirically observable conditions, and it is necessary to treat them as such. From the fact that there are heart attacks one may conclude that it is impossible to be sure, *a priori*, that a given heart is healthy or not, but only a sophist would conclude that it is impossible to tell a healthy heart from a diseased heart. "Istae dubitationes stultae sunt", St. Thomas Aquinas says tranquilly, "and one is worth as much as another, since they have a common source. These sophists seek to prove everything. It is obvious that what they want is to be furnished with some principle which will serve them as a sort of rule to distinguish the healthy man from the sick one, the live man from the dead one. And yet they will not be content with a simple knowledge of the rule; they must have it strictly proven to them."

All one can do for them is to prove that everything cannot be proven. Now, to demand a proof of the truth of empirical distinctions obvious to everyone is to demand a proof of a principle; let us respond with Aristotle: "Rationem quaerunt quorum non est ratio, demonstrationis enim principium non est demonstratio."[11]

Let us hold fast to this precious formula. It is impossible to demonstrate sensation because it is itself a principle. In order to understand the realist position and accept it in its purity, it is necessary to recall that, in the order of existential judgments, sensible perception has the nature and value of a principle of knowledge. Descartes contributed more than a little to the eclipse of this principle by propagating the illusion that there are no other principles than those of pure thought, even in Aristotle's philosophy which he opposed. Since he himself admitted no other principles he naturally supposed that sensation was not a principle for Aristotle either, which left classical realism with no other principle than the abstract concept of being. From that point on Descartes had good reason to reproach the scholastics for wasting their time in sterile contemplation of a principle from which there could be no escape. But there is in Aristotelianism, in addition to the first principle which regulates all judgments, a first source of all knowledge, and that is sensation.

That is the true meaning of the formula which is so often cited but is so rarely accepted in its full rigor, namely, that nothing is in the understanding unless it has first been in the senses. "Nothing" applies to everything, even the content of the first principles of simple apprehensions and of judgments: being and the principle of contradiction. This is expressly

[11] St. Thomas Aquinas, *In IV Metaph.*, lect. 15 (Cathala ed.), n. 708-10. For Aristotle's formula, cf. *Métaphysique* 4, 6, 1011a 13.

affirmed by St. Thomas: "Omnis nostra cognitio originaliter consistit in notitia primorum principiorum indemonstrabilium. Horum autem cognitio in nobis a sensu oritur."[12] But to admit the truth of this formula is still not necessarily to understand it. The magic spell cast by idealism is such that almost every modern reader will immediately conclude from these words that if a man were not actually perceiving a sensible object the intellect would be unable to formulate a first principle which it nevertheless contains within itself and has the right to apply to other beings. Actually, it is precisely in its own light that the intellect formulates the first principle, but it borrows its content from the sensible datum.

Whatever anyone else may think on this question, there can be no doubt as to what Aristotle thought. For him, as one of his translators and commentators justly remarks: "The logical impossibility of both affirming and denying a predicate of a subject at the same time is based upon the ontological impossibility of the coexistence of contraries." That is exactly what the following text of the *Metaphysics* implies: "There are philosophers, as we have said, who claim on the one hand that the same thing can both be and not be and, on the other hand, that this is conceivable. As for us, we have already indicated that it is impossible for the same thing to both be and not be, *and it was by this means that we demonstrated that this principle is the most certain of all.* "[13] This is

[12] St. Thomas Aquinas, *De Veritate*, q. 10, a. 6, Praeterea.

[13] Aristotle, *Métaphysique* 4, 4, 1005b 35–1006a 5. Cf. J. Tricot's translation, 1:123 and n. 1. This passage is so obscurely translated in the *translatio media* that St. Thomas himself thought about the problem in his commentary on the passage: *In IV Met.*, lect. 6 (Cathala ed.), n. 606. Although he had not read this passage, St. Thomas understood the doctrine thoroughly, as can be seen from what he says about actual existence as the cause of truth.

the true Aristotelian tradition, and it is also the one and only foundation upon which a true realism may be based. All truth, including the first principle, is imposed upon thought as necessary because it is first necessarily so in the order of being. This is because, in itself, what is cannot not be, so that it is impossible for us to think that what is is not.

What is true of the first principle itself is equally true of judgments made in light of it concerning every object of sensible perception in general. This is why the senses, the first principle of the content of the first principle, are at the same time the first principle of all real knowledge. We might say that our judgments are made between two extremes: sensation and the intuition of intellectual principles. This is what Aristotle says,[14] and St. Thomas repeats it in a text that is all the more instructive because in it he is responding directly to the objection based upon dreams and hallucinations.

In his eyes, what distinguishes a dream from a judgment made while awake is that, in the latter case, the judgment is formed in the light of two opposite principles: the intellect, which plays a role in both cases, and sensation, which is lacking in the first. In other words, the judgment of the dreamer may well be connected to the first principle as conceived, but he has no perceived first principle to support his judgment. In short, since the *resolutio ad sensum* cannot be carried out, our knowledge lacks one of its principles. This is not real knowledge at all; rather, it is an internal sensation or a play of imagination.[15]

---

[14] Aristotle, *Nicomachean Ethics* 6, 8, 1142a 25–29.

[15] "Sed quia primum principium nostrae cognitionis est sensus, oportet ad sensum quodam modo resolvere omnia de quibus judicamus; unde Philosophus dicit in III *Coeli et Mundi* quod complementum artis et naturae est res sensibilis visibilis, ex qua debemus de aliis judicare; et

Thus, no matter in what manner nor with what profundity we may pose the question as to how we know that something exists, realism will always respond: by perceiving it. Here we find ourselves led to the point in the problem at which it must be conceded that realism is at least coherent. How is the apprehension of existence possible for man, a knowing subject endowed with understanding and sensation? To the question thus framed there can be no question as to whether we are speaking of existence itself or merely the knowledge we have of it.

The earlier objection raised by certain neo-Thomists who contend that there is no existential index is effectively eliminated by the preceding analysis. It is dismissed by St. Thomas as sophistical, a fact which should at least give Thomists pause for thought. Since sensation bears witness to existence we have no need of any other existential index than the certainty which accompanies sensation. That one who is no longer in possession of this criterion should be exposed to error is hardly surprising. While he is asleep the dreamer does not know that he is dreaming, but when he awakes he realizes that he was dreaming. It would be tragic indeed if philosophers philosophized in a dream: that is what realists, at least, seek to avoid.

---

similiter dicit in VI *Ethic.* (cap. VIII in fin.), quod sensus sunt extremi sicut intellectus principiorum; extrema appellans illa in quae fit resolutio judicantis. Quia igitur in somno ligati sunt sensus, non potest esse perfectum judicium nisi quantum ad aliquid, cum homo decipiatur intendens rerum similitudinibus tamquam rebus ipsis; quamvis quandoque dormiens cognoscat de aliquibus quod non sunt res, sed similitudines rerum" (St. Thomas Aquinas, *Quaest. disp. de Veritate*, q. 12, a. 3, ad 2). Cf. loc. cit., ad 3. For St. Thomas, the real difficulty is not to know how the dreamer can mistake images for perceptions but how the dreamer can, in certain cases, *not* mistake these images for perceptions.

There is no real difficulty with our knowledge of existence, any more than there is a problem of existence itself. Moreover, complementary explanations and clarifications of this point now come to the fore, and they show us what vast fields of psychological exploration are offered to realists if they will busy themselves with resolving their own problems instead of becoming lost in labyrinths that nobody need enter. If we view the whole problem of the existential judgment as it should henceforth be presented to us, it is in fact reduced to describing the complex act by which man apprehends the existence which his mind conceives but does not perceive and which his senses perceive but do not conceive.

An examination of certain expressions used in everyday speech will suffice to reveal the general outlines of the problem posed by the existential judgment. When I say "I see a man" or "I perceive the existence of this table", the least reflection will allow us to see how inaccurate expressions of this kind are. I can neither see nor perceive "man" or "existence", since they are concepts. What I really mean to say is that I know, by means of my intellect, that what was perceived with my senses is a man or an existent. However, confused as they may be, expressions like this give a marvelous idea of the complex unity of psychological experience, for that is what we are dealing with here. When the problem of the apprehension of a sensible being by a human *conjunctum* is raised, we are immersed in experience from beginning to end. Therefore, it will suffice for our purposes to say that we spontaneously express our perceptions in accordance with the way we experience them, that is, as perceptions of an intelligent subject, and the formulation of our judgments is governed by the manner in which we come to know their terms, as concepts charged by sensible images and often still closely associated with sensations. In short, man knows what he senses and senses what he knows.

The direct observation of these facts of internal experience is its own justification. If we go on to cite St. Thomas Aquinas, it is only to assure those who wish to rework classical realism after their own fashion that their predecessors did not wait for the twentieth century to state these self-evident truths. St. Thomas' technical language need not concern us as long as we perceive the reality he is speaking about. Psychologists are free to use different language to express their further observations; St. Thomas at least had the good sense to call attention insistently to the important fact that human understanding is the act of a human intellect and that man's sensations are the operations of human sensibility.

Animal sensibility is already much more than a passive recording of sense impressions. The behavior of animals proves that they are capable of acquiring a purely sensible experience and, up to a certain point, of adapting themselves to their surroundings. This ability sometimes seems to mimic the operations of reason. The ability to combine and organize images into a series enabling the animal to act in a manner appropriate to the circumstances was called *aestimativa* in the Middle Ages. To the extent that he is himself an animal, man also has this capability; it frees the voluntary activities from the need to perform acts which, in normal circumstances, the body can accomplish far better than the reason. However, medieval philosophers often gave man's *aestimativa* capability a distinct name; they called it *cogitativa* or even *ratio particularis,* not at all because it has a reasoning function in man, but because it functions in man as the sensibility of an intelligent being. The expression *ratio particularis,* a confusing term that expresses the community of function in the unity of a single subject, indicates that just as man's memory can perform functions which an animal's cannot, so too man's sense powers can perform functions even more similar to reason than an animal's. Why? Because, says St. Thomas, our sensibility possesses *aliquam affinitatem et propinquitatem ad rationem universalem, secundum quamdam refluentiam*.[16] The expressions are deliberately vague; today it is psychology's task to give them a more precise content. What concerns us is the fact itself: the osmosis which occurs between sense and intellect in the unity of the knowing human subject.

As might be expected, the reverse of this phenomenon is also produced: to the intellectualization of the senses by the understanding there corresponds a "sensibilitization" of the understanding by means of the senses. This is what certain frequently repeated adages of the schools intend to say, but few understand their true meaning. It is not enough to say: "it is impossible to think without a phantasm"; we must understand that what we conceive with the intellect is presented to us through and in the data of sense experience. Just as the object perceived is knowable but is ignored by the intellect, so also the sensible species is laden with an intelligibility which the senses cannot grasp. Indeed, intelligibility is to be found nowhere but in the sensible species. We are not separate Intelligences thinking Platonic Ideas. Sensible beings exist separately and independently of each other, but intelligibles do not exist apart from sensibles. This is why St. Thomas says that the intelligibles of the human intellect are in the sensible species *secundum esse*. We grasp the intelligible in the sensible because it exists there. If we wish to learn anything, we first need a sense impression. If we wish to think and reflect about something

[16] St. Thomas Aquinas, *Summa Theologica* I, q. 78, a. 4, ad 5.

we already know, we must return to the sensible images we already possess.[17]

Taking the foregoing into consideration, it is easy to see how the problem was reduced to the formula cited so freely by contemporary Cartesio-Thomism: *intellectus est universalium, sensus vero singularium*. The formula is most assuredly true, but it is not necessary to read it as if we were dealing with a Cartesian understanding separated from a Cartesian sensibility in some "Cartesian Man" composed of Thought united to a Machine. That is what all those do who, while professing with St. Thomas and Aristotle that man is the substantial unity of soul and body, pose the problem of knowledge as if they did not know that man's body exists and who attempt the impossible task of establishing a link between the material world and a disembodied soul. In a coherent realism the problem is not presented in this way. The intellect knows universals, but it knows them only in a phantasm. Thus, in the last analysis, intellectual knowledge of universals requires the perception of singulars. This is why, in a sense, man acquires a certain intellectual knowledge of the singular and can even use his reason, within limits, to return to the special characteristics of the individuals he encounters.

In order to accomplish this intellectual grasp of the singular, the *ratio particularis* places organic groups of phantasms at his disposal, and their often subtle texture bears witness to the empirical sensitivity of intelligent being. Let the man thus enriched by this mutual interpenetration of sense and intellect immerse himself in his experience; let him leave to his understanding the task of expressing what it has just become. Then we will see his old concepts narrow their

---

[17] St. Thomas Aquinas, *In III de Anima*, lect. 13 (Pirotta ed.) n. 791.

scope to express this new object and become supple so as to
fit its contours until finally a suitable word will flow forth
from the depths of thought. This is what our whole being
has awaited. Certainly this word may still not convey perfectly the singularity it was intended to express, but of all
conceivable words it will have expressed it best. Thus, as St.
Thomas says, the mind is able to grasp the particular in its
own fashion: *mens singularia cognoscit,* first by a reflective effort that allows it to recover, in the concept, the image and
sensation from which it was drawn out, and then by the
natural movement of the soul, which is toward beings,
seeking to be united with them. St. Thomas' language on
this point bears hardly any resemblance to the language of
critical realism. Thought, he tells us, "*Continuatur viribus
sensitivis* . . . secundum quod motus qui est ab anima ad
res, incipit a mente, et procedit in partem sensitivam, prout
mens regit inferiores vires; *et sic singularibus se immiscet* me-
diante ratione particulari, quae est potentia quaedam in-
dividualis quae alio nomine dicitur cogitativa, et habet
determinatum organum in corpore, scilicet mediam cellu-
lam capitis."[18] This certainly resembles Descartes' pineal
gland, but Descartes was concerned with a Thought, not
with a soul. Thought cannot mix with sensible beings,
which is why Descartes wrote five metaphysical meditations
in order to demonstrate the existence of the external world,
a fact he otherwise would never have doubted.

Thus, for St. Thomas the problem of the existential judgment is linked to the analogous problem of the apprehension
of the singular. It could hardly be otherwise in a doctrine in
which only individuals exist. If we review what the understanding grasps *immediately* at the moment of sense perception,

[18] St. Thomas Aquinas, *Quaest. disp. de Veritate,* q. 10, a. 6, ad Resp.

we will have a list of the cases in which, although it knows the universal, the intellect can be said to *see*. The Thomist position is quite clear on this point. It is a question of what, *ad occursum rei sensatae, apprehenditur intellectu*. For example, if I hear someone speak or see him move, I know immediately that he is alive; I may therefore say that I see that he is alive: "Apprehendo per intellectum vitam ejus, unde possum dicere quod video eum vivere."[19] Likewise, if I happen upon some individual or animal, my practical reaction will not be governed by their general nature, for I see them as being this particular individual or animal. Animals do not have this sensible knowledge of "the individual perceived as belonging to a general class", but particular reason gives us this knowledge, "quia vis sensitiva in sui supremo participat aliquid de vi intellectiva in homine, in quo sensus intellectui conjungitur."[20]

In a doctrine in which man, in a way, conceives the singular and perceives the universal because in their constant and instantaneous exchanges thought and sensation collaborate in the unity of the same act, intellectual knowledge is just the opposite of the empty, abstract thought of which Aristotelianism has been accused. Far from being reduced to a pure logical form, in Aristotelianism the concept is always conceived in and by means of the concrete. In fact, what is criticized under the heading of scholastic abstraction is actually a caricature of true realist abstraction, for it neither contains the empirical content which Aristotle attributed to it nor does it retain its simple nature, as maintained by Descartes. Cartesio-Thomism's mistake is to believe that a monster which could only be of interest to philosophical teratology is viable. Once you start with a realist notion of

[19] St. Thomas Aquinas, *In II de Anima*, lect. 13 (Pirotta ed.), n. 396.
[20] Ibid., n. 397.

abstraction it is futile to seek to reunite abstraction with an object which it presupposes. If you feel that abstraction should not presuppose its object, it would be far better to stop treating it as an abstraction, since there is no longer anything from which it could be abstracted. Make it the idea of some Cartesian thought, but do not try to play two tables at one time. Realist abstraction is an apprehension of the universal *in* the particular and of the particular *through* the universal. The concepts and judgments it utilizes substitute for our lack of an intellectual intuition of the singular. Since we are men we are unable to apprehend being in the way a pure spirit would, but we are able to apprehend being as men, grasping it as closely as possible through the union of our intellect and our sensibility.

CHAPTER EIGHT

THE APPREHENSION OF EXISTENCE

If we are agreed that man is the only real knowing subject and that the apprehension of existence belongs in the class of apprehensions of the singular, then we must also seek to determine how the apprehension of existence differs from other members of this class. This difficult undertaking seems to have led certain realists to become involved in critical philosophy. Thus they made a difficult task impossible, for when a problem concerning being arises, only metaphysics, not the critique, can offer a solution. Now, we have seen that the Cartesio-Thomists seek a critical justification for metaphysics; it therefore becomes necessary for them to explain how it is possible to apprehend existence before knowing what existence is. Since there is no reason for us to invert the normal order of these questions, we will first ask what the word "existence" means and only then seek to know whether, and if so, how, what it means may be apprehended.

All critical realists agree without discussion that existence is not a sensible quality. From this they immediately infer that existence cannot be perceived by the senses. Both propositions are true but, as we have seen, they are not the whole truth. Likewise, realists who claim to be in the Aristotelian tradition all agree that being is the first principle of intellectual knowledge, but they do not always agree as to how to formulate this principle, nor do they always agree concerning the reality it expresses. Some maintain that the first principle is the principle of identity, others that it is the principle of contradiction. If it be granted, however, that there is a good chance that St. Thomas knew the meaning of his own teaching, we may be forgiven for leaving the neo-Thomists to their controversies and instead asking the mentor they all claim as their own what he has to say on the subject.

As a matter of fact, St. Thomas approaches the problem in a different way. What he says about being is so clear, when his formulations are taken in their full meaning, that none may doubt for a single moment the manner in which, for him, the human intellect apprehends the most immediate of its objects. Most writers never tire of citing the formula St. Thomas borrowed from Avicenna in which he says that being is the first thing encountered by the intellect.[1] But the terms St. Thomas uses to describe the apprehension of being are not sufficiently remarked upon. This first of all the objects of thought presents to the greatest degree the character of being apprehended immediately through contact with sensible things. We will have further occasion to remark upon this characteristic later. Now, we have just studied the nature of intellectual apprehensions of this sort. They form the class St. Thomas calls "sensible by accident".

---

[1] "Primo in intellectu cadit ens, ut Avicenna dicit . . ." St. Thomas Aquinas, *Metaphysics* I, lect. 2 (Cathala ed.) n. 46. Cf. "Dicemus igitur quod ens et res et necesse talia sunt quae statim imprimuntur in anima prima impressione, quae non acquiritur ex aliis notioribus se." Avicenna, *Metaphysics* tr. 1, chap. 6, fol. 72b A. Other analogous citations: "Illud autem quod primo intellectus concipit quasi notissimum, et in quo omnes conceptiones resolvit, est ens, ut Avicenna dicit in principio Metaphysicae suae" (bk. 1, c. 9) (St. Thomas Aquinas, *De Veritate* q. 1, a. 1, resp.) Cf. *Metaphysics* 10, lect. 4 (Cathala ed.), n. 1998; 11, lect. 5, n. 2211.

This means that, although they are intelligible in themselves, the objects of these apprehensions are in a way seen, that is, sensed, because no intellectual operation is interposed between their conception and the sensible preception in which the intellect apprehends them.

This much is certain, then, from the beginning of this new inquiry: the apprehension of being by the intellect consists of directly seeing the concept of being in some sensible datum. For the moment, let us try to clarify the nature of what it is that the intellect apprehends when it conceives the first principle. To begin with, we must distinguish two operations of the intellect. The first, which is simple, is the means by which the intellect conceives the essences of things; the other, which is complex, affirms or denies these essences of one another and is called judgment. In each of these two orders there is a first principle: being, in the order of apprehension of essences, the principle of contradiction in the order of judgments. Moreover, these two orders are arranged hierarchically, for the principle of contradiction presupposes the understanding of being: "Hoc principium, impossibile est esse et non esse simul, dependet ex intellectu entis." Thus, the principle which is first in the order of simple apprehensions is also absolutely first, since it is presupposed by the principle of contradiction itself. In short, the first principle, in the fullest sense, is being.[2]

---

[2] "Ad hujus autem evidentiam sciendum est quod, cum duplex sit operatio intellectus: una, qua cognoscit quod quid est, quae vocatur indivisibilium intelligentia: alia, qua componit et dividit: in utroque est aliquod primum, quod cadit in conceptione intellectus, scilicet hoc quod dico ens; nec aliquid hac operatione potest mente concipi, nisi intelligatur ens. Et quia hoc principium: impossibile est esse et non esse simul, dependet ex intellectu entis, sicut hoc principium: omne totum est majus sua parte, ex intellectu totius et partis: ideo hoc etiam principium est naturaliter primum in secunda operatione intellectus, scilicet

Here a serious difficulty arises. What is this being that the intellect apprehends? St. Thomas tells us that it is the first thing encountered by the intellect in the order of *quod quid erat esse.* Therefore, it would seem that we are in the order of essences. But if what the intellect apprehends is only, so to speak, the essence of existence, then this is not the very act of existing which is grasped. Therefore, actual existence eludes the intellect, and we thus return to the same difficulty we had hoped to eliminate: the intellect, the faculty concerned with universals, never grasps concrete existence in its singularity. This objection is not faked for the sake of the argument; it is imposed by the texts. It is true by definition that the object of the *intelligentia indivisibilium* is essence. As St. Thomas says, following Aristotle, the understanding of indivisibles "consistit in apprehensione quidditatis simplicis". Or again: "intellectus habet verum judicium de proprio objecto, in quod naturaliter tendit, quod est quidditas rei"; but the quiddities, or essences, apprehended by the intellect have no other existence than an existence in the reason: "Quidditatis esse est quoddam esse rationis."[3] To say that we attain being only as existing in the reason is to admit that our intellect is, from the very beginning, cut off from the existential order as such. Not only does the first principle not attain existence, it does not even see it. How then can the intellect attain a grasp of existence

---

componentis et dividentis. Nec aliquis potest secundum hanc operationem intellectus aliquid intelligere, nisi hoc principio intellecto. Sicut enim totum et partes non intelliguntur nisi intellecto ente, ita nec hoc principium omne totum est major sua parte, nisi intellecto praedicto principio firmissimo" (St. Thomas Aquinas, *Metaphysics* bk. 4, lect. 6 [Cathala ed.], n. 605).

[3] Thomas Aquinas, *In I Sent.,* 19, 5, 1, ad 7.

by some further operation, since by its very nature it depends upon this principle?

To resolve the problem we must first point out that the difficulty did not escape the notice of the classical realists. By that I mean to say that they did not confuse abstract being, conceived by thought, with the actual being of objects *quae secundum esse totum completum sunt extra animam.* Therefore, supposing that Aristotelianism has failed in its undertaking, it is not because it was mistaken on this point. On the contrary, perhaps it is we who have mistaken the nature of existence and as a consequence have also been mistaken concerning the conditions that would make existence knowable to us. Existence escapes the senses, for they are only able to perceive certain sensible qualities and group them into stable associations. What the senses perceive exists, and existence is included in what the senses perceive, but the senses are only the bearers of a message which they are incapable of reading, for only the intellect can decipher it. However, the intellect alone cannot decipher it completely. What it is able to read in the sensible datum is the answer to the question: what is this?

Now, the answer to the question *quid* is the quiddity, which is to say: the definition which indicates *quid est res.* This definition, or quiddity, is the essence apprehended by the intellect in the sensible datum, and this is why philosophers substitute the term "quiddity" for "essence". Thus, in our knowledge of the external world the intellect immediately apprehends the essence of its object insofar as it is revealed to the intellect by the sensible effects it causes. Therefore, if we admit that the word "nature" designates the essence of a being insofar as it governs the actions that the being accomplishes and which our senses perceive, we may say that we perceive sensible quiddities or natures by means of the intellect. But this essence is not in itself our answer to the question *quid*; it is the definition of our answer to the question. Likewise, the essence is not primarily the principle of a being's operations; rather, it causes the being to act only because it first causes the being to exist. "Essentia dicitur secundum quod per eam et in ea res habet esse."[4]

To get to the bottom of this analysis of the concrete we must therefore go beyond a simple description of its elements in order to grasp their function. Since *essentia est secundum quam res dicitur esse,* the essence by which a being composed of matter and form is said to exist must necessarily include both matter and form. However, although the essence includes both, the two do not play the same role in the composition, for what causes being, or essence, is form. Thus, the quiddity which the intellect defines contains the essence which the quiddity defines. The essence, in its turn, contains the form, the cause of the being of the existent, and the act by which form causes something to exist is the very heart of reality. The term used to describe this matters little, as long as we understand that we are here dealing with that whose intrinsic perfection not only is the cause of existence but at the same time is the cause of every other perfection. One might say that all the rest is in potency with regard to the existential energy of the form, because it is the cause in virtue of which all the rest exists. That fire or a man should exist is certainly a perfection, but beyond the fact that "a certain thing exists" is the fact of existence, pure and simple. Thus understood, the act of existence is seen by the realist as the ultimate source of what causes experience: "Esse est inter omnia perfectissimum"; or again, "hoc quod dico *esse* est actualitas omnium actualitatum, et propter hoc

---

[4] Thomas Aquinas, *De Ente et Essentia,* chap. i, last sentence.

est perfectio omnium perfectionum." When this or that particular being is offered to knowledge in sensible experience, the intellect does not apprehend existence *plus* what makes it this or that particular being. A certain "manner of existing" consists of nothing more than existing in a certain manner. In short, the way in which a thing exists is blended, for this particular thing, with its proper mode of existing. As for being itself taken in its pure actuality, it cannot be the object of a natural experience: it is God.

In such a realism of knowledge, itself integrated with a realist metaphysics, the fact that a certain being is categorized as falling into a particular form of existence is simply an expression of the particular type of limitation which constitutes its intelligibility. This is why St. Thomas says, in a vigorously worded text, that the differences between forms can be distinguished only if their matter is used by way of specific difference. For a form is act insofar as it is form; therefore, it is part of being and, since it is impossible to add to being something which is not itself being, it is impossible to distinguish one existential actuality, as such, from another actuality. Forms owe their differences to the limitation of their existential act by matter. For example, how can we distinguish the act which is the soul from all other acts? By specifying that the soul is the act of an organized body susceptible of life.[5] Thus, the quiddity formulated by a

[5] Ad nonum dicendum, quod hoc quod dico esse est inter omnia perfectissimum: quod ex hoc patet quia actus est semper perfectior potentia. Quaelibet autem forma signata non intelligitur in actu nisi per hoc quod esse ponitur. Nam humanitas vel igneitas potest considerari ut in potentia materiae existens, vel ut in virtute agentis, aut etiam ut in intellectu; sed hoc quod habet esse, efficitur actu existens. Unde patet quod hoc quod dico esse est actualitas omnium actuum, et propter hoc est perfectio omnium perfectionum. Nec intelligendum est, quod ei quod dico esse, aliquid addatur quod sit eo formalius, ipsum determinans,

definition marks the point at which the intellect comes in contact with existential reality, which we conceive in and through the definition, and in no other way.

This explains the seeming opposition which many historians have pointed out between two theses whose Thomist character is beyond dispute. On the one hand, quiddities are the natural object of the intellect; on the other hand, essences are unknown to us.[6] The opposition is only

---

sicut actus potentiam; esse enim quod hujusmodi est, est aliud secundum essentiam ab eo cui additur determinandum. Nihil autem potest addi ad esse quod sit extraneum ab ipso, cum ab eo nihil sit extraneum nisi non ens, quod non potest esse nec forma nec materia. Unde non sic determinatur esse per aliud sicut potentia per actum, sed magis sicut actus per potentiam. Nam et in definitione formarum ponuntur propriae materiae loco differentiae, sicut cum dicitur quod anima est actus corporis physici organici. Et per hunc modum hoc esse ab illo esse distinguitur, in quantum est talis vel talis naturae. Et per hoc dicit Dionysius (cap. V, *De Div. Nom.*, non remote a princ.), quod licet viventia sint nobiliora quam existentia, tamen esse est nobilius quam vivere: viventia enim non tantum habent vitam, sed cum vita simul habent et esse. Thomas Aquinas, *De Potentia* q. 7, a. 2, ad 9. Cf. *Summa Theologica*, I, q. 4, a. 1, ad 3. *Quaest. disp. de Anima*, a. 6, ad 2. *Quaest. quodlibetales*, Quodlib. 9, a. 3, resp.

[6] Cf. for example G. Rabeau, *Species Verbum: L'Activité intellectuelle élémentaire selon S. Thomas d'Aquin* (Paris: J. Vrin, 1938); 152–53, in which this agnosticism is expressed in the most precise terms. Moreover, the author adds that, no matter how you interpret it, St. Thomas could not have expressed himself in this manner by mistake. To which we will add that, although quiddity is essence insofar as it is knowable and definable by us, the term can sometimes be used to designate the essence; but St. Thomas avoids this when dealing with the question of whether we can know essences. Thus, St. Thomas writes *De spiritualibus creaturis*, a. 11 ad 3, "quod formae substantiales per seipsas sunt nobis ignotae." G. Rabeau tells us that "the response to the seventh objection . . . says the exact opposite" (op. cit., 151, n. 5). Here is that response: ". . . duplex est operatio intellectus. . . . Una qua intelligit quod quid

apparent. Each time St. Thomas affirms that essences and substantial forms are unknown to us, he never fails to add something like: "Innotescunt autem nobis per accidentia propria." The opposite is also true: when he speaks of a knowledge of essences, he is thinking about the knowledge we have of their quiddity. In this sense we can speak of the human intellect understanding and even comprehending an essence, but this is not a direct intellectual intuition of the essence in its pure actuality; rather, we understand an essence insofar as we perceive it in its actions. Insofar as it is manifested in its sensible effects, the essence is the quiddity, for this is what we know as the essence, and this is what we use to formulate a definition in answer to the question *quid*.

Therefore, it is simultaneously true to say both that essences are unknown to us and that we conceive them. They are unknown because the form which confers their intelligibility upon them is itself purely intelligible. Now, pure intelligibility escapes our intuition; therefore, *per seipsas*, they are unknown to us. But we conceive them because they are present in their sensible effects, which we perceive and from which our intellect abstracts them as quiddities. Classical realism is based upon the double fact that our knowledge truly attains reality because reality is the cause of our knowledge and that, even if our knowledge is not an intuition, it attains reality as it really is because our intellect grasps what is intelligible in reality, thanks to our sensibility. Thus, St. Thomas agrees with Kant in denying that man has an intellectual intuition of things in themselves,

---

est: et tali operatione intellectus potest intelligi essentia rei . . ." (op cit., a. 11 ad 7). The understanding of an essence by understanding the quiddity does not contradict the fact that substantial forms are, for us, unknowable *per seipsas*. On the contrary, the one thesis implies the other.

but he maintains, while Kant denies, that our knowledge by means of concepts does attain reality as it really is, although it does not exhaust the intelligibility of reality in the way an intuition would.

This is why, in the final analysis, realism is an all-or-nothing proposition. The touchstone of realism is its definition of man's essence as "rational animal", and our knowledge is established as real by the existential act which makes the essence exist as what it is. It is not enough to give mere verbal assent to the proposition that truth is an adequation of understanding and being. To give this formula its full realist meaning, we must go beyond the schema in which a being is reduced to an essence, which is itself reduced to the quiddity expressed in the definition. St. Thomas' whole noetic invites us to go beyond that, and he himself said so in so many words, although it must have appeared self-evident to him: a being's act of existence, not its essence, is the ultimate foundation of what we know to be true about it. Now, it so happens, by a good luck which is not entirely a matter of chance, that the example chosen by St. Thomas is precisely that of the concept of existence: "Cum autem in re sit quidditas ejus et suum esse, *veritas fundatur in esse rei magis quam in ipsa quidditate,* sicut nomen entis ab esse imponitur; et in ipsa operatione intellectus accipientis esse rei sicut est per quamdam similationem ad ipsum, completur relatio adaequationis, in qua consistit ratio veritatis."[7]

We thus find ourselves led on to the question whose answer we are seeking, and it is now possible to see where the answer will be found. In order for man to perceive being with his intellect, an existent must be given to him, an existent perceptible to his sensibility. Therefore, it would be

---

[7] Thomas Aquinas, *In I Sent.* dist. 19, q. 5, a. 1, Sol.; ed. Fr. Madonnet, 1:486.

incorrect to pose the problem only from the point of view of the existential judgment, for before we can affirm existence it is necessary to apprehend it. It would be equally incorrect, however, to seek the cause of our knowledge of the existence of some object in a *species intelligibilis* of actual existence. Whatever intelligible species the intellect is provided with, it can only conceive universals. But the intellect is able to see being in the sensible objects we perceive. The continuity of sense and intellect in the knowing subject permits us to do this. Now, it is certain, and everyone can prove this for himself, that our idea of being is often accompanied only by vague images, sometimes even by verbal images alone, which do not direct the judgment to any concrete existent. At other times we think of objects as existents, but without doing more than applying the abstract concept of existence to images which represent the objects. However, when the concept of being is abstracted from a concrete existent perceived with the senses, the judgment which predicates being of this existent attributes being to it according to the way it is conceived by the intellect, namely, as "seen" in the sensible datum from which it is abstracted.

Here we discover the true realist meaning of the formula: *ens est quod primum cadit in intellectu*. With its first thrust the intellect apprehends what is most profound in its object: the *actus essendi*. But we do not encounter Pure Being in experience; we encounter the being of concrete substances whose sensible qualities affect our senses. Therefore, one could say that existence accompanies all our perceptions, for we are not able to directly apprehend any other existents than those with sensible quiddities, and we cannot apprehend them other than as existing. Experience is a witness to the fact that this is what happens. Is it so difficult, then, to understand that the concept of being is presented to knowledge as an intuitive perception since the being conceived is that of a sensible intuitively perceived? The existential acts which affect and impregnate the intellect through the senses are raised to the level of consciousness, and realist knowledge flows forth from this immediate contact between the known object and the knowing subject.

Thus, it is only by means of a fundamental fallacy that anyone can claim to reduce classical realism to some sort of "mediatism". Such a position would maintain that a whole series of intermediaries intervene between the object and the intellect and that sensibility separates the intellect from beings. The human intellect can no more exist apart from the man whose intellect it is than human sensibility can. If the knowledge with which we scrutinize nature is the knowledge of a man, we have a solid reason for saying that nothing is interposed between the knowing subject and the known object. Now, what is true of all real knowledge, that is, of all knowledge concerning actually existing concrete subjects, is eminently true of our knowledge of their existence. For since the *actus essendi* has no opposite except nothing, there is no middle course between knowing existence and knowing nothing. The intellect is able to abstract from the known object one or the other of its constitutive elements in order to consider that element separately, or to separately consider what is left of the object after abstracting that element. We can, for example, conceive of the form of a substance apart from its matter or even define its matter apart from its form. In both instances we obtain a distinct and intelligible concept; but how can we think about all or part of a substance apart from being? If it is not being, it is nothing, and we will have nothing left to think about. Thus, we must necessarily conclude that, if knowledge of existence is abstractive, it is an abstraction inseparable from the existence from which it is abstracted.

Considered from this point of view, the labors and anxieties which certain realists impose upon themselves in order to do justice to what they believe to be sound in idealism would appear to be doomed to remain fruitless. To intend to think as an idealist is to intend to think the unthinkable. It is therefore hardly surprising that idealists themselves do not succeed in doing so. If being is the first object of the understanding, it must be the first object of all human understanding without exception. This is so true that every refusal to accept being where it is found necessitates that it be found where it is not. When a man refuses to think as a realist when he should, he is inevitably condemned to think as a realist when he should not. In fact, and this is one of the most precious lessons we can learn from history, the philosophical experience proves that every idealist interpretation of reality doubles as a realist interpretation of our knowledge of reality.

This is what happened to Descartes, who, having refused to start with material beings posited as existing, was immediately constrained to posit Thought as a substance and to treat the ideas in which it participated as beings endowed with their own objective reality. If Descartes had not reified these abstractions he would have had nothing left to think about, neither within nor outside himself; from its first step, his philosophy would have been immersed in nothingness. Thus, he constructed the phantasmagorical world of "simple natures" in which he led his philosophical life and in which every realist who follows the same path is condemned to live also. Berkeley's Spirits are phantoms with the same origin as the Cartesian Thoughts, for although the reality of bodies ceased to exist for the bishop of Cloyne, his pure spirits absorbed their substance and, since they could no longer borrow their ideas from an external world of things, they perceived as beings what they said were only ideas. As Berkeley repeated so many times, things are what we perceive them to be because our ideas *are* the things. His naive philosophy believes it has saved the world from what he calls Descartes' and Locke's skepticism by solving the problem of the connection between knowledge and reality with a simple suppression of reality. It will then be necessary to relocate reality so that it will be within knowledge. What gives Berkeley's experiment its special interest is that it is the most naive realism of thought the world has ever known.

From the moment one leaves the precincts of realism, he is condemned to commit the sophism which, by modifying slightly A. N. Whitehead's justly famous formula, we might call the "sophism of the misplaced existence". From this perspective the whole history of philosophy, to the extent that it bears upon this problem, may be divided in two: natural realism on the one hand and, on the other hand, every conceivable variety of idealist error under whatever form it may be expressed. What is called Platonic idealism is the same as what was called realism during the Middle Ages, and what was called realism in the Middle Ages has the same origin as what is called idealism today. Having begun by discrediting sensible reality, nearly reducing it to the status of nonbeing, Plato and Plotinus were forced to attribute the reality which they denied sensible being to something else. Thus their irrealism of the real world was paralleled by a realism of an unreal world. The medieval realism of Ideas or Universals was merely the counterpart of a certain lack of realism in the sensible order. Moreover, this is why historians visibly hesitate to call the Platonic realism of ideas an idealism; whichever term is used it is simply a question of using two words to describe the same philosophical error. There is only one realism worthy of the name and

THE APPREHENSION OF EXISTENCE

that is the one which consists of attributing existence to what exists and not attributing it to what does not exist. The precise nature of Plato's Ideas, Avicenna's Natures, Descartes' Thoughts or Berkeley's Spirits matters little; we are basically concerned with one phenomenon: apart from the natural realism of classical Aristotelianism, there are only inverted realisms.

The exceptional importance of Kant's work stems from the fact that he brought out this essential characteristic of all dogmatic idealism. Henceforth, what could be called the idealist inversion would appear as a simple disease of natural realism, resulting in his decision to dismiss all speculation of this sort as foreign to philosophical knowledge. This is why, having liberated himself from all dogmatisms, Kant decided to seek in the study of the *a priori* conditions of thought the means of securing a firm foundation for knowledge by limiting it. The result was a critical idealism, that is, one purged of all hypotheses concerning the ultimate nature of reality in itself and firmly determined not to burden itself with any responsibility in this regard.

Taken in itself, and granting the initial decision which forms its basis, critical idealism is an intelligible philosophical position. To the extent that it remains faithful to its essence, as for example in Léon Brunschvicg's philosophy, it is perfectly coherent and renders the service its defenders expect of it: the radical elimination from philosophy of all realism, whether normal realism or inverted realism. But realism cannot be eliminated from thought itself because the contact with reality from which knowledge flows cannot be eliminated. This is why the realism eliminated from philosophy by the critique still remains in knowledge, but it is reduced in critical idealism to the infraphilosophic condition of a common-sense realism. We are thus led to the following paradoxical result: a philosophy in which the fact that the external world exists is stripped of all importance since, although there is no doubt that it exists, this whole philosophy acts as if it did not exist. Therefore, critical idealism can only attain its end by coming to terms with a realism in which it refuses to become involved. Its resolute purity requires it to share in the benefits of an enterprise whose expenses it refuses to share. First of all, the critical realist lives in two radically different universes: as a man he uses the resources of one world that the professor of philosophy gains by teaching a different world. But the philosopher also gains the benefits of living in two worlds at the same time. The critical idealist is careful not to deny that the external world exists because if he did he would fall into Berkeley's metaphysical idealism, but he does not seem to see that by accepting critical idealism he must also accept the metaphysical realism of common sense. As Kant said, since there are appearances there must be beings which appear. This makes excellent sense, but anyone who accepts this reasoning becomes entangled in an existential realism which differs from Aristotle's realism only in its refusal to consider itself an object of philosophical reflection, even if only to render itself intelligible by understanding itself.

Thus, critical idealism avoids a metaphysics of existence only by decreeing that the fact that there is a world of objects known and of knowing subjects is of no philosophical significance. Nevertheless, it is necessary for critical idealism to go even farther down this curious path of philosophical detachment. Just as philosophers of the judgment do not mistake themselves for simple collections of judgments formed by judgmental faculties other than their own, so also critical idealists do not reduce the world of bodies whose existence they accept to an *x* eternally hidden in the shadow of the phenomena. Since they accept its existence, critical idealists at least grant that the external world is knowable and even that it lends itself to such knowledge. The least that can be said for the Fichtean "shock" is that it is an intelligible shock and, just as the woodcutter knows that wood splits well only with the grain, the scientist knows better than anyone that empirical reality has a fibrous structure: progress in the understanding of reality can only be made by following the paths of intelligibility. Certainly reason often anticipates experience, but reason can only foresee something as a function of what is already known. No one, I think, would deny the reality of the reciprocity between reason and experience; it is the warp and the woof from which science is woven.

Since critical idealism is a reflection upon knowledge, it presupposes knowledge: knowledge and its conditions. Thus, critical idealists must at least admit that beings must be of such a nature that they are able to be known and that the knowing subject must be of such a nature that it is able to know them. It is possible to ask what makes knowledge possible; this inquiry opens the problem of the "ontology of knowing"[8] and leads epistemology to its natural end: metaphysics. By deciding to confine itself to a reflection upon the *a priori* conditions of science, critical idealism shows a sure instinct for self-preservation, for it declares that metaphysical problems are insoluble only while also holding that they have been resolved. How can we argue in the name of justice against one who recognizes justice only when he can derive some benefit from it? And how can we reason with a critical idealist in the name of the metaphysics whose validity

[8] It is hardly necessary to recall here the excellent book published by M. Y. Simon under this title.

he denies, when all the while he accepts without discussion truths which only metaphysics can make known? Critical idealism mistakes its profession of ignorance for a profession of wisdom. One who blasphemes that of which he is ignorant is too human even to reproach.

The situation in which philosophy found itself after Kant cannot be described as a pure and simple substitution of idealism for realism. Behind every idealism can be found a naive realism. The only difference is that, instead of looking for a rational explanation that would render it intelligible to itself, this realism is henceforth entrenched in its essential naiveté. The realism of a critical idealist is naive by its very vocation. There is no question of a rift within his philosophy, but this internal coherence presupposes a total breach between his philosophy of knowledge and the knowledge in virtue of which it is called philosophy, since his philosophy is based upon a common-sense knowledge which is forbidden him insofar as he is an idealist. A philosophy conditioned upon a completely unintelligible condition is a completely arbitrary philosophy, which all the evidence urges us to reject.

If what we have said is true, the opinion advanced in certain neo-scholastic schools that idealism is inevitable, at least as regards method, must arise from some misconception concerning the true nature of philosophy. Some tell us that there must be a problem concerning the existence of the external world, since certain philosophers say there is. True, but this problem is posed only by philosophies which, having denied the self-evidence of the external world, have attempted the impossible task of proving its existence. Thus, the problem only becomes a problem at the moment when the actual existence we are seeking has been lost forever. Why, then, has this problem been raised? Because of an error in method which realism must oppose because realism is itself the true method.

The starting point of idealism can hardly be said to be immediately evident. In fact, no idealist principle of knowledge is posited as immediately evident. Each of them is discovered only at the end of a reflexive analysis which leads the prisoners from the cave to the light of day: the Cartesian by purifying himself from the uncertainty of sensation with the certitude of the *cogito*, the Kantian by liberating himself from Hume's skepticism with the *a priori* conditions which serve as a ground for the necessity of judgments. In each case the discovery of the idealist first principle is conditioned by an analytic reflection whose ultimate end is erected as the first principle of knowledge. This method has become so important in the eyes of modern philosophers that they identify it, under the name "reflexive method", with the normal conduct of philosophical reflection. Certainly every philosophical inquiry is reflexive, but the method called reflexive is different from a simple reflection. It consists of making the ultimate end of an analytic reflection the necessary and sufficient condition of the reality analyzed. If, as has been seen, intellectual knowledge is an abstractive knowledge, the reflexive method undertakes to posit what the understanding retains from reality as the necessary and sufficient cause of what is eliminated during the course of its regressive analysis. Such a method is sophistical and replete with impossibilities of all sorts.

It is sophistical because it consists of transforming a concept caused in us by external being into an idea which will itself be a cause. The reflexive method, therefore, presupposes that, in virtue of being ultimate, a concept becomes generically different from that from which it is abstracted. The idealist then finds himself confronted with an inevitable choice: he can either unjustifiably transform the concept into an idea, thus entering the realm of idealist metaphysics, or he can repudiate the concept and the idea after having repudiated external reality. The latter course leads to critical nihilism, the normal end of an idealist method faithful to the spirit that inspired it. The modern philosophies of judgment are perfect examples of this nihilism, since they retain no more of reality than the pure acts connecting the absences of intelligible terms whenever unintelligible "shocks" occur, the origins of which are unknown. Judgments without concepts are conceivable in a nominalism of the sensible intuition, such as Ockham's, but once sensible intuition is discredited, this position reduces philosophy to a reflection which is nourished on itself: *chimaera bombinans in vacuo comedens secundas intentiones.* The contemporary philosophy of judgment is far more sterile than anything known to the Middle Ages. It spends its time chasing after science, which takes next to no notice of it and expresses only mild appreciation for the belated approbation these philosophers give to what is already becoming scientifically out of date.

Why do realist philosophers become involved in this sort of game? If they do, they will either have to load the dice by pretending to discover the existence of the external world, a fact which they never doubted, or else they will have to attempt seriously to prove what is self-evident and as a consequence end up destroying it. Now, for a realist to try to work with an idealist's tools is to renounce his own. The realist's craft consists, first, of upholding the truth of the first principles against all comers; next, of bringing these principles out into the light of day to reveal their self-evidence and, finally, of describing the nature of these principles in order to assign them their proper places in the edifice of human knowledge. Only then will a realist epistemology, based upon the intrinsic evidence of its principles and the agreement between these principles and reality, be possible.

An honest philosophical disagreement is much better, we maintain, than an illusory agreement which inevitably degenerates into sheer confusion. Some claim to see in the desire for purity which animates every true realism an intentionally extremist policy and an obsession with exaggerating the differences between realism and idealism. The real question is whether these differences *can* be exaggerated! How could it be possible to exaggerate a disagreement concerning the very nature of the first principles of knowledge? No conceivable disagreement could be more absolute than that between two positions, one of which accepts human knowledge as it is while the other rejects it for one reason or another. The disagreement between realism and idealism is absolute; it is therefore necessary to call a spade a spade. For if what we have said is true, we should do all in our power to make it known. Philosophy does not consist of encouraging others to continue in false beliefs, and the worst way of persuading others to abandon their error is to appear to share the same error. There is only one truth, the same for all, and the highest good for a rational being is to know the truth. When a philosopher sees the truth he can only submit himself to it, for that is true wisdom; and when he has discovered the truth, the best thing he can do for others is share it with them, for that is true charity.